Portland's Little Red Book
of
Stairs

❦ Stefana Young

Foreword by Dr. Moira Gunn

First edition. Copyright © 1996 by Stefana Young.

Printed in the United States of America
Library of Congress Card Catalog # 96-092986

Published by Coobus Press

Send inquiries to:
Coobus Press
P.O. Box 15085
Portland, OR 97239
(503) 234-8265 FAX (503) 232-3511

Cover designed by Chris Gagnon

Printed by Lazerquick Copies® Portland, OR
Portland Center
Michael Kelley
Bob Baker

ISBN #0-9655418-7-8

Every effort has been made to provide accurate and current information, but the information in this book is not guaranteed. Neither the author nor the publisher will assume any responsibility for its use.

Dedication

This book is dedicated to my father,

Evan Rowland Williams.

He was one great walker.

Table of Contents

Foreword

So, why would I write a foreword to a book about stairs? What do they have to do with technology? First of all, because stairs are technology. In fact, when you think about it, risers and treads represent some of the earliest forms of technology ever —maybe just after fire and right before the wheel....

I bet you've been taking stairs for granted.

I'm here to tell you that while you have been ignoring stairs, they may have played an important part in your life. When I was a child, every Christmas morning my brother and I would run to the second-floor landing in my parents' house and squint through the railing, looking down at the Christmas tree. "Did Santa come?" we would yell to our parents, and then spill down the stairs as fast as we could. I can still remember every step, every turn, every creak.

There have been stairs that I regularly said good night to boyfriends on, stairs on which I sat and chatted with my friends, stairs that I climbed to receive diplomas, stairs that I taught my own children to climb up and down, and stairs on which I stopped and had a moment alone.

When you think about it this way, the stairs in your life suddenly come alive.

And just like your life, if you look at Portland through its public stairs, a whole new city will come alive before your eyes. You'll find rambling gardens and magnificent vistas, local history and abandoned dreams, hidden paths, antique light posts, charming gates and more. There are stairs made of metal and cement and wood and railroad ties and dirt.

And you will realize that many hands and minds and hearts built Portland, and it is truly a living city.

Dr. Moira A. Gunn
Producer & Host
Tech Nation ... Americans & Technology
Heard weekly in Oregon on
National Public Radio

Introduction

Jewett Park Stairs

Introduction

A plaque in a tiny Portland Heights park reads, "There is nothing like sitting on steps in the sun when one has the unparalleled pleasure of doing just nothing at all."

But what about the exhilarating pleasure of ascending 287 stairs to the top of Mt. Tabor? If the climb doesn't take your breath away, the view of the west hills will. Then there's the quiet pleasure of walking down a set of stairs and discovering a hidden garden or a forgotten memorial.

But that is the nature of stairs — they are seats for pondering and challenges for the taking. Stairs are great for Slinkys. However you choose to approach the step, it's alive and living in Portland. The City of Portland maintains over 165 stairways. The Portland park system must see to the welfare of at least 50 sets of stairs. There are also many stairways up and around the Willamette River bridges that require tending. When all is tallied, Portland has an excess of 9,000 stairs steps.

The sheer number of stairs throughout Portland is somewhat meaningless, however, unless you understand that vertical thoroughfares are woven into the historic fabric of Portland. In 1895, Portland Heights residents were tied to the stairs as a method to get to and from the trolley stops. In the early 1900's, several stairways were built along "The Alameda" in Northeast Portland to provide pedestrians with direct access to the flatlands. Planners of "City Park," now Washington Park, employed stairs to infuse grandeur into an entrance. The original City Park stairs, the stately stone stairs up to the Amphitheatre and the Rose Gardens stairs elevate the splendor of the landscape.

Introduction

The Oregon Resource Directory

Portland has long been nationally recognized as a leader in historic preservation. Evidence of this commitment to Portland's past is in the creation of the Oregon Resource Directory. The 10-volume body of work is the result of four years of searching out and classifying properties in Portland that might be of historical and architectural significance. The intent of the inventory is to, "...protect scenic and historic areas and natural resources for future generations and promote healthy and visually attractive environments in harmony with the natural landscape character." The properties — all 5,000 of them — have been ranked with this goal in mind. The ranking does not mean that the properties are necessarily designated landmarks. The ranking should be thought of as a notation that the property has been evaluated and has met certain criteria.

Twenty stairways in Portland have been named in the Oregon Resource Directory. They are all considered historically significant as architectural landscaping. Their Rank III standing tells us that the stairways, "...add richness and character to the neighborhood."

The Oregon Resource Directory has been a wonderful resource for this book, adding color and texture to the stairs by connecting them to Portland people and places. Many of the historic anecdotes in the book are pulled from the Directory. Many "factoids" are derived from it. The Directory is a treasure and one of the most influential components of this book.

Introduction

The Artists

Portland artist Barbara Stafford is currently showing her extensive body of work in galleries all along the West coast, including San Francisco and Portland. Her pen drawings of such subjects as the Japanese stairs, the birdhouse with bamboo and many more add an inspired dimension to the book.

Rhonda McHugh is also a Portland artist and is well known for her expressive and lively water colors. Her choice of subjects is varied, from PGA golf professionals to animals. Rhonda is currently working on a "Series of Grace." Grace is both a model mother and a mother model.

Photography

The photographs in this book come from several sources. The historical photographs were printed with the permission of the Oregon Historical Society. Sarah Williams, my sister, contributed photographs. My cousin, John Williams, was the primary photographer for the Northwest Hills. He also provided me with a camera and gave me crash course on framing shots, f-stops, etc.

Point of Departure

All directions in the book start from Pioneer Courthouse Square. Recognized as a public square and unofficial heart of Portland, Pioneer Courthouse Square also seems fitting as a point of departure. First of all, it's got lots of stairs. At the risk of insulting any courthouses, I refer to Pioneer Courthouse Square as Pioneer Square in the directions.

In addition to written directons, each stair entry has its own Thomas Guide reference information so if you're equipped with a Portland version, you're in good shape. Otherwise, any city map will do just fine in locating the stairs.

Introduction

Buster

Buster is my black cocker spaniel and research assistant. Every step I've taken on the stairs, he's taken four. Buster is my buddy. He's never complained about my penchant for stairs, or at least I don't think so. Buster is mentioned regularly in the text and heavily featured in photographs. If it seems odd to have a mongrel as a muse, I suggest you pick up the *The Blue Dog* by artist/writer, George Rodrigue. At least my dog is still alive.

Buster. A dog. A black dog. Buster.

Acknowledgments

I'm one lucky person. I have talented friends and colleagues that don't seem to mind being mercilessly exploited for my own gain. Eric and Chris Gagnon put me through book publishing boot camp in "The Flophouse," and I am forever indebted to them. Robin Davis Corrigan's editing skills are keen and her gardening knowledge is unmatched. She is exceptional in many ways but mostly she's my dearest friend. Barbara Stafford reignited my excitement for this project when I sat at her kitchen table and watched her in action. She possesses a generosity of talent and spirit and I am truly grateful for her contributions. Rhonda McHugh also jumped right into the fray and dusted off her pen and inks for me. Her painting style breathed life into concrete. Many thanks. Janis Grout saved me with her great caption quips and she cleans windows too. John, Nancy and Matthew Williams were not only helpful with photography but they also proved to be great models. Also thanks to Uncle David and Aunt Donna for their ongoing encouragement. Many thanks also to David R. Davis for just the right word when my brain failed me. And thank you Counselor Charles E. Corrigan for legal minutia and general nitpicking.

Two years ago, Bill Hoffman, manager of Pedestrian Transportation, got me started with a hefty gift of stair inspection reports. The reports were bequeathed to me with only one proviso; I had to write a book about stairs within a year or he'd have the job done in-house. Sorry Bill. It took two years. Thanks for your patience.

My original partner in crime was my sister, Sarah Williams-Fay. While our collaboration was geographically impossible, Sarah has pledged ongoing support throughout the process. My entire family has been wildly supportive and I thank them. Marilyn Williams, in particular, came in very handy with her computer skills. Her readiness to help knows no bounds.

The library staff at the Oregon Historical Society is also to be commended. The "Third Floor" gang is consistently upbeat, always helpful and resourceful. I must also thank Bob Downing, Pat Billings and Phil Wortman.

And last but never least, always first, I thank my husband, George. He indulges me in my wild schemes and makes me laugh.

Southwest Portland *Washington Park*

Washington Park Stairs

Southwest Portland *Washington Park*

Washington Park

Washington Park is the pride and joy of the Portland Public Parks system. The Washington Park Zoo, Hoyt Arboretum, the Rose Garden and Japanese Garden and Vietnam Memorial attract hundreds of thousands of visitors every year. The rolling terrain of Washington Park also makes it home to some incredible stairways. And they're all different. Some are wonderfully dilapidated, others are bold and stately entrances to gathering spots like the Washington Park Amphitheater.

A walk in the park was an almost daily ritual when I lived just off the main park entrance. I would wander about the Park, discovering one hidden staircase after another. Of course, the vistas and plant life are spectacular and the stairs are beautifully woven into the lay of the land.

Of the three entrances to Washington Park, the West Burnside entrance is considerably more isolated than the other park entrances. This now, lesser-known entrance is an occasional meeting place for devotees of fortified spirits. That also tends to be the case for the S.W. Madison entrance. And yet, both areas are still frequented by scores of dog walkers, nature lovers, romantic couples and runners. One time I was heading into the park from West Burnside with Buster, and we were met by a trio of men crouched on the side of the hill, imbibing in a bag 'o booze. They smiled, waved and went about their business. I smiled, waved back and continued along without incident. Park officials say there are efforts to discourage vagrant activity in the park. The only word of caution would be to avoid walking on the north side of the park after dusk.

West Burnside was originally Washington Street. The north side of the park was also the original main entrance for what was then called City Park (from 1871 to 1904). After almost 10 years of political wrangling and general dillydallying by park board members, city officials and the mayor, City Park was changed to Washington Park in 1912.

Southwest Portland *Washington Park*

"The Coming of the White Man"

West Burnside Street up to the "The Coming Of The White Man" statue
Year Built: Around 1900
Number of Stairs: 278
Top Locator: "The Coming Of The White Man" statue
Bottom Locator: W. Burnside St. entrance by Stearns Memorial
Thomas Guide: 596, C-5

Directions: From Pioneer Square (S.W. Broadway and S.W. Morrison St.), take S.W. Morrison St. west to S.W. 10th Ave. Turn right on S.W. 10th Ave., then turn left on W. Burnside. Go up W. Burnside about a mile, past N.W. 23rd Ave. Right across the street from the west parking lot of Uptown Shopping Center are pedestrian entrances into Washington Park. Look for the Loyal B. Stearns Memorial. To the right, past the paved road, you'll find the modest beginnings to a very long set of stairs.

❦ This venerable staircase appears to be the oldest of the three staircases found on the north side of Washington Park. What at first appears to be a trot up some steps quickly turns into a relentless trudge. The stairs and trail vary so it's never a bore. You'll find flagstone risers here, cobblestone ones there. The several landings en route must accommodate old gnarled trees that, over the years, have slanted the stairs and landings this way and that. Watch your step. Upon reaching the top of the stairs, you'll be met by "The Coming Of The White Man" statue. Created in 1904, this full-size bronze sculpture depicts two early native Americans grimly looking out towards the east. One gets the distinct impression that they're none too pleased.

Southwest Portland *Washington Park*

West Burnside Street up to Lewis and Clark Circle
Year Built: Unknown
Number of Stairs: 178
Top Locator: Lewis and Clark Circle
Bottom Locator: Corner of W. Burnside St. and S.W. Osage St.
Thomas Guide: 596, C-5

Directions: From Pioneer Square (S.W. Broadway and S.W. Morrison St.), take S.W. Morrison St. west to S.W. 10th Ave. Turn right on S.W. 10th Ave., then turn left on W. Burnside St. Go up W. Burnside St. about a mile, past N.W. 23rd Ave. Right across the street from the west parking lot of Uptown Shopping Center, look for the Loyal B. Stearns Memorial. At the Stearns landmark turn to the left and follow the S.W. Osage St. sidewalk. The beginning of the stairway will be directly ahead.

❦ This set of stairs is one of the longer, more challenging climbs in Washington Park, although the landings and dirt and gravel paths break up the action. The first set of stairs takes you up to a path. Follow this path to the next set of steps up to the left. There's one more connecting path and then the final 103 stairs will take you up to Lewis and Clark Circle.

Southwest Portland *Washington Park*

W. Burnside Street up to Washington Park Access Road
Year Built: Around 1900
Number of Stairs: 50
Top Locator: Paved pedestrian access road
Bottom Locator: W. Burnside entrance by Stearns Memorial
***Thomas Guide*:** 596, C-5

Directions: From Pioneer Square (S.W. Broadway and S.W. Morrison St.),
take S.W. Morrison St. west to S.W. 10th Ave. Turn right on S.W. 10th Ave.,
then turn left on W. Burnside St. Go up W. Burnside St. about a mile, past
N.W. 23rd Ave. Right across the street from the west parking lot of Uptown
Shopping Center is the Loyal B. Stearns Memorial. Walk about 100 yards up
the center walkway and the stairs will be on the right.

❦ This stairway goes quite unnoticed if you're walking way up the park path
and it's virtually impossible to miss if you're heading back down to W.
Burnside St. These steps are really old, really dilapidated and really don't
lead anywhere. Still, it's one of those I-wish-I-was-a-photographer settings —
a perfect composition of mossy, weather-beaten, slanted stairs, set against a
lush backdrop of greener-than-green fern tendrils and a strategically placed
slug.

The forgotten stairs in Washington Park.

Southwest Portland *Washington Park*

Buster strikes a pose on the old main entrance stairs.

Southwest Portland *Washington Park*

W. Burnside Street up to Lewis and Clark Circle
Year Built: Around 1900
Number of Stairs: 39
Top Locator: Lewis and Clark Circle
Bottom Locator: Loyal B. Stearns Memorial
Thomas Guide: 596, C-5

Directions: From Pioneer Square (S.W. Broadway and S.W. Morrison St.), take S.W. Morrison St. west to S.W. 10th Ave. Turn right on S.W. 10th Ave., then turn left on W. Burnside St. Go up W. Burnside St. about a mile, past N.W. 23rd Ave. Across the street from the Uptown Shopping Center west parking lot is the Stearns Memorial. The walkway begins right behind the Memorial.

❦ This walkway is gracefully flanked by still-operable light posts from a bygone era. Towards the conclusion of the path, you'll happen upon a set of 39 steps. That's right Mr. Hitchcock. At the top of the stairs is a brick building that houses restrooms (open seasonally). You'll also see S.W. Wright Ave. skirting the west side of the park.

Southwest Portland *Washington Park*

Greeting from City Park in Portland, Ore. 1915

Greetings from Washington Park 80-plus years later.

Southwest Portland *Washington Park*

S.W. Park Place up to Lewis And Clark Memorial
Year Built: Around 1905
Number of stairs: 25 stairs
Top Locator: Lewis and Clark Obelisk
Bottom Locator: Washington Park Main Entrance
Thomas Guide: 596, C-6

Directions: From Pioneer Square (S.W. Broadway and S.W. Yamhill St.),
take S.W. Broadway south to S.W. Taylor St. and turn right or west. At S.W.
17th Ave. make a left, then a quick right onto S.W. Salmon St. (two-way
street here). Go up the hill past the Multnomah Athletic Club. The road
takes a little jog at S.W. King where it turns into S.W. Park Pl. Go straight up
S.W. Park Pl. past the S.W. Vista intersection and you'll literally run into the
stairs.

❦ This is a great stairway if only for the fact that you're afforded an up-close
look at these exquisitely manicured flower and shrub beds. According to
City of Portland Rose Curator Bob Downing, the design and plant varieties
change from year to year. They currently feature santolina planted and
pruned into an extraordinary "Greek Key" pattern that's worthy of applause.

❦ The park entrance stairs lead you up to the 20-foot high granite obelisk
commemorating the arrival of Lewis and Clark to the Pacific Coast in 1805.
Teddy Roosevelt lay the cornerstone for the monument in May of 1903 and
the project was finished in time for the 1905 Lewis and Clark Exposition.
Other public works of art that shouldn't be missed in Lewis and Clark Circle
are "Sacajawea" and the cast-iron fountain. Sculptor Alice Cooper was
commissioned to create "Sacajawea" for the 1905 Exposition and the statue
was unveiled in a ceremony that featured speakers Susan B. Anthony and
Abigail Scott Duniway. After the Exposition festivities, the statue was moved
to Washington Park. The cast-iron fountain on the west side of the circle was
created in 1891, a replica of a fountain from the Renaissance era. The
original statue was topped by a small boy holding a shaft. The figure took an
unfortunate tumble during a routine cleaning and did not survive the fall.

Southwest Portland *Washington Park*

The reservoir promenade made for a lovely walk in the park in 1915.

"Fountain in City Park, Portland, Oregon" 1914

Southwest Portland *Washington Park*

S.W. Madison Street up to Upper Reservoir
Year Built: Around 1915
Number of Stairs: 64
Top Locator: S.W. Madison Washington Park entrance
Bottom Locator: Lewis and Clark Circle
Thomas Guide: 596, C-6

Directions: From Pioneer Square (S.W. Broadway and S.W. Yamhill St.), take S.W. Broadway south to S.W. Taylor St. and turn right or west. At S.W. 17th Ave. make a left, then a quick right onto S.W. Salmon St. (two-way street here). Go up the hill past the Multnomah Athletic Club. The road takes a little jog at S.W. King Ave. where it turns into S.W. Park Pl. Turn left onto S.W. Vista Ave. Turn right onto S.W. Madison St., the street right before you cross Vista Bridge. Just as you enter the park on S.W. Madison St., you'll see the foot path to the stairs on the left side of the road.

❦ As you go up the foot path, you'll see some stairs to the right that lead to a grassy landing. You have the option of taking these stairs and meeting up with the reservoir stairs after a mild bushwhack up an ivy hill. You may also stay on the path that will lead to another flight of stairs. Either way, the next set of stairs will take you up to Lewis and Clark Circle.

❦ The two reservoirs in Washington Park were originally designed to function as promenades with stairs leading down to the walkway around the reservoir. Reasons for the eventual fencing off of the area vary from tragic drownings to an LSD water-spiking scare.

Southwest Portland *Washington Park*

The stately stone Amphitheatre entrance gives off a sense of grandeur.

Camellia Circle is a tranquil island of greenery.

Southwest Portland *Washington Park*

S.W. Rose Garden Way up to the Main Amphitheatre Entrance
Year Built: 1930
Number of Stairs: 28
Top Locator: Amphitheatre entrance
Bottom Locator: Camellia Circle
Thomas Guide: 596, C-6

Directions: From Pioneer Square (S.W. Broadway and S.W. Yamhill St.), take S.W. Broadway south to S.W. Taylor St. and turn right or west. At S.W. 17th Ave. make a left, then a quick right onto S.W. Salmon St. (two-way street here). Go up the hill past the Multnomah Athletic Club. The road takes a little jog at S.W. King Ave. where it turns into S.W. Park Pl. Go past S.W. Vista Ave. and straight up into Washington Park. Follow the signs to the Rose Gardens. The main entrance to the Amphitheater is about halfway up S.W. Rose Garden Way. No parking is available until further up the hill.

❧ The development of Washington Park Amphitheatre has been a gradual effort since the acreage was first designated as an amphitheatre in 1925. The stone stair entrance was built in 1930. The concrete seating wall was built in 1975 and a permanent stage was erected in 1979.

❧ Just across the road from these stairs is another point of interest, an isolated island of greenery called Camellia Circle. The tranquility of the Circle generates inexplicable desires to put dandelions in one's hair and macrame a plant holder.

Southwest Portland *Washington Park*

Take center stage any time at the Washington Park Amphitheatre.

Southwest Portland *Washington Park*

S.W. Rose Garden Way down to Amphitheatre Stage
Year Built: Around 1930
Number of Stairs: 64
Top Locator: West Amphitheatre entrance
Bottom Locator: Amphitheater stage
Thomas Guide: 596, C-6

Directions: From Pioneer Square (S.W. Broadway and S.W. Yamhill St.), take S.W. Broadway south to S.W. Taylor St. and turn right or west. At S.W. 17th Ave. make a left, then a quick right onto S.W. Salmon St. (two-way street here). Go up the hill past the Multnomah Athletic Club. The road takes a little jog at S.W. King Ave. where it turns into S.W. Park Pl. Go past S.W. Vista Ave. and straight up to Washington Park. Follow the signs to the Rose Gardens. The west entrance to the Amphitheatre in on S.W. Rose Garden Wy., just north of the restrooms.

❦ These stairs in the Amphitheatre branch out to several landings that are used for concert seating, picnicking or just hanging out. You'll also see other sets of stairs lining the perimeter of the audience area that are fair game for climbing. When you get to the bottom of the stairs, hop up on the platform and take a big, sweeping Rose Festival curtsy.

Southwest Portland *Washington Park*

S.W. Rose Garden Way down to Queen's Walk
Year Built: 1917
Number of Stairs: 90
Top Locator: Main entrance to Rose Garden
Bottom locator: Queen's Walk
Thomas Guide: 596, C-6

Directions: From Pioneer Square (S.W. Broadway and S.W. Yamhill St.), take S.W. Broadway south to S.W. Taylor St. and turn right or west. At S.W. 17th Ave. make a left, then a quick right onto S.W. Salmon St. (two-way street here). Go up the hill past the Multnomah Athletic Club. The road takes a little jog at S.W. King Ave. where it turns into S.W. Park Pl. Go past S.W. Vista Ave. and straight up to Washington Park. Follow signs to the Rose Gardens. The middle entrance to the garden is found on S.W. Rose Garden Way, just south of the Amphitheatre entrance.

❦ The first set of stairs from the street level will lead you down to the International Rose Garden Test Center kiosk. The next succession of stairs, just below the kiosk, will take you down to the Queen's Walk. While you're tap dancing on the plaques of yesteryear's Rose Festival Queens, check out the penmanship of some of these Queens. Alas, the art of cursive writing is dead. Looking out to the east is a picture-perfect postcard setting with the city in the foreground and Mt. Hood in the distance.

❦ The Rose Gardens in Washington Park are the oldest, continuously operated public rose test gardens in the United States. The gardens were founded in 1917 by leading American rose nurserymen. The group was in search of an alternate locale for their European rose test gardens, closed due to World War I. Much to the excitement of Portland city officials, our town was selected from among several competing cities for the honor of becoming the new site for the International Rose Test Garden.

Southwest Portland *Washington Park*

S.W. Rose Garden Way down to South Queen's Walk
Year Built: 1917
Number of Stairs: 56
Top Locator: South Rose Garden entrance
Bottom Locator: South end of Queen's Walk
Thomas Guide: 596, C-6

Directions: From Pioneer Square (S.W. Broadway and S.W. Yamhill St.), take S.W. Broadway south to S.W. Taylor St. and turn right or west. At S.W. 17th Ave., make a left, then a quick right onto S.W. Salmon St. (two-way street here). Go up the hill past the Multnomah Athletic Club. The road takes a little jog at S.W. King Ave. where it turns into S.W. Park Pl. Go past S.W. Vista Ave. and straight up to Washington Park. Follow the signs to the Rose Gardens. The south entrance to the rose garden is just across the street from the south set of tennis courts.

❦ The first 21 stairs from the street level will take you down into the Rose Garden. Turn to the left towards the Frank L. Beach Memorial Fountain. Erected in 1975, the sculpture commemorates the man who nicknamed Portland the "City of Roses." The stairs to the left of the sculpture feature beautiful arches of climbing roses over each landing.

*The Frank L. Beach Memorial Fountain reminds us that
Portland will always be the "City of Roses."*

Southwest Portland *Washington Park*

S.W. Rose Garden Way up to Tennis Courts
Year Built: Unknown
Number of Stairs: 30 (North Set) 19 (South Set)
Top Locator: S.W. Kingston Tennis Courts
Bottom Locator: S.W. Rose Garden Wy.
Thomas Guide: 596, C-6

Directions: From Pioneer Square (S.W. Broadway and S.W. Yamhill St.), take S.W. Broadway south to S.W. Taylor St. and turn right or west. At S.W. 17th Ave. make a left, then a quick right onto S.W. Salmon St. (two-way street here). Go up the hill past the Multnomah Athletic Club. The road takes a little jog at S.W. King Ave. at which time it turns into S.W. Park Pl. Continue on S.W. Park Pl. past S.W. Vista Ave. and enter Washington Park. Follow signs to the Rose Gardens. Once you're at the top of S.W. Rose Garden Way, the Rose Garden will be to the east of you and a row of six tennis courts are to the west or just above you.

❦ There are two set of stairs, one to the south and one to the north, that will take you up to the courts for a quick game, set, match. The Washington Park tennis courts are equal opportunity and tennis whites are far from required. Any time of the day, weather permitting, you can witness the full spectrum of tennis acumen.

S.W. Kingston up to the Washington Park Zoo Train Platform
Year Built: 1961
Number of Stairs: 44
Top Locator: Washington Park Zoo Train platform
Bottom Locator: S.W. Kingston shelter
Thomas Guide: 596, C-6

Directions: From Pioneer Square (S.W. Broadway and S.W. Yamhill St.), take S.W. Broadway south to S.W. Taylor St. and turn right or west. At S.W. 17th Ave. make a left, then a quick right onto S.W. Salmon St. (two-way street here). Go up the hill past the Multnomah Athletic Club. The road takes a little jog at S.W. King Ave. where it turns into S.W. Park Pl. Continue past S.W. Vista Ave. on S.W. Park Pl. and enter Washington Park. Follow signs to the Rose Gardens. Take S.W. Rose Garden Wy. past the Rose Gardens to where the street meets up with S.W. Kingston Ave. The stairs to the Washington Park Station platform are to the east or left of the shelter.

❦ The Washington Park Zoo train has been a favorite of Portlanders, both young and old, since the first Zooliner began chugging around the zoo grounds in 1958. That was a full year prior to the official opening of the zoo. Plans were always in the works to expand the train route out to Washington Park, funding permitting. Money was raised and the Washington Park station platform was dug out of the hill in 1960. The station building itself was taken from the 1959 Centennial celebration grounds. The stairs and tunnel leading to train platform were not built until July of 1961.

❦ The round trip of the Washington Park Zoo train is approximately four miles and takes about 35 minutes. According Jeff Honeyman, train buff, zoo volunteer extraordinaire and part-time engineer, the three trains that make up the Washington Park Zoo train fleet, collectively carry a staggering 350,000 people a year.

Southwest Portland *Washington Park*

These stairs are located along the gravel trail that takes you up to the main entrance of the Japanese Gardens. While there may be a sameness to the dirt treads terraced by smooth round logs, the depth of each stair demands that the walker choose between either taking an elongated stride or opting for the two-step per stair approach. Either way, the irregular length heightens our awareness of the path.

S.W. Kingston up to the Japanese Garden
Year Built: Around 1962
Number of Stairs: 15
Top Locator: Main entrance to Japanese Garden
Bottom Locator: S.W. Kingston Ave. entrance to Japanese Garden
Thomas Guide: 596, C-6

Directions: From Pioneer Square (S.W. Broadway and S.W. Yamhill St.), take S.W. Broadway south to S.W. Taylor St. and turn right or west. At S.W. 17th Ave. make a left, then a quick right onto S.W. Salmon St. (two-way street here). Go up the hill past the Multnomah Athletic Club. The road takes a little jog at S.W. King Ave. where it turns into S.W. Park Pl. Go straight up S.W. Park Pl. and enter Washington Park. Follow the signs to the Japanese Garden.

❦ The Japanese Garden in Washington Park is a true horticultural treasure. Covering over five and a half acres, the Japanese Garden has been drawing crowds ever since it first opened in 1962. The "idealized conception of nature" in each of the five gardens — Tea Garden, Strolling Pond Garden, Sand and Stone Garden and Flat Garden — arouses a keen reverence for the great and the small.

❦ The presence of the step or stair is an important architectural element in the Japanese garden. The stair is both understated yet structurally decisive. Most successions of stairs are rarely uniform; a small stepping stone may be followed by a flat slab of aggregate concrete that could lead to flagstone steps. The irregularity of materials, shapes and sizes of the steps compels us to watch our step. In doing so, we slow down our pace. In this new frame of mind, we're more inclined to take in the details on the ground — a brilliant green tuft of moss clinging to a rock or a small ceramic clay symbol inlaid on a step. In achieving this more relaxed state, we are better able to embrace the true harmony of the surroundings.

Southwest Portland *Arlington Heights*

A 1927 Mediterranean-style home hovers above the base of the stairs.

This Frank Lloyd Wright-like house has a commanding view of the city.

Southwest Portland *Arlington Heights*

S.W. Marconi Avenue up to S.W. Kingston Avenue
Year Built: Unknown
Number of Stairs: 74 (Including S.W. Parkside Lane)
Top Locator: S.W. Parkside Dr.
Bottom Locator: S.W. Marconi Ave.
Thomas Guide: 596, C-6

Directions: From Pioneer Square (S.W. Broadway and S.W. Yamhill St.), take S.W. Broadway south to S.W. Taylor St. and turn right or west. At S.W. 17th Ave. make a left, then a quick right onto S.W. Salmon St. (two-way street here). Go up the hill past the Multnomah Athletic Club. The road takes a little jog at S.W. King Ave. where it turns into S.W. Park Pl. Continue S.W. Park Pl., past S.W. Vista Ave., and up into Washington Park. Follow the Lewis and Clark Circle around to the right and stay right on S.W. Park Pl. DO NOT follow the signs to the Rose Gardens and Japanese Garden. About a block later, S.W. Marconi Ave. begins at right-angles to S.W. Park Place. The stair trek begins here.

❦ At the S.W. Marconi Ave. street sign you'll see a low stone entrance with four flagstone stairs. These stairs meet up with a cobblestone path that takes you up to four more stairs before reaching an open grassy lawn. Direct yourself straight across the lawn to a gravel path that makes a hairpin turn up to the right. Follow it and you'll hit a set of hidden concrete stairs. Go up the stairs to an alley of sorts, S.W. Parkside Dr. If you go to the left, you'll be at the corner of S.W. Kingston Ave. and S.W. Parkside Dr. The tennis courts, Rose Garden, Amphitheatre, etc. are just to the left. If you go to the right, the street narrows into an alleyway between some huge houses on either side. Just at the end of the alley there's another flight of stairs that takes you down to S.W. Tichner Dr.

❦ This is a great little trek that takes you away from the madding crowd and ambles up the hill in a most curious way. The first set of stairs and the subsequent cobblestone path are very slippery when wet. Take care.

Southwest Portland *Arlington Heights*

Vertigo sufferers need not apply for these stairs.

Southwest Portland *Arlington Heights*

S.W. Champlain Drive up to S.W. Fairview Boulevard
Year Built: Unknown; Rebuilt: 1987
Number of Stairs: 80
Top Locator: 2933 S.W. Fairview Blvd.
Bottom Locator: 2864 S.W. Champlain Dr.
Thomas Guide: 596, B-5

Directions: From Pioneer Square (S.W. Broadway and S.W. Morrison St.), take S.W. Morrison St. west to S.W. 10th Ave. Make a right and then a left onto W. Burnside St. Go up W. Burnside St. past Uptown Shopping Center and make a left at the second light past N.W. 23rd Ave. There's a left turn lane onto S.W. Tichner Dr. Take S.W. Tichner Dr. up the hill. At the stop sign, turn right on S.W. Kingston Ave. At the next stop sign, turn right onto S.W. Fairview Blvd. The next street to your right is S.W. Rutland Ter. Make another right. S.W. Rutland Ter. will meet up with S.W. Champlain Dr. as you continue up the hill. Begin looking for the 2864 address on the left side of the street.

❦ The Champlain-Fairview stairs go past a splendidly well-planned terraced garden. The residents of the cheery yellow house have taken full advantage of the available plots of soil on either side of the stairway. The tender-loving hands of a gardener are clearly evident here. Fragrant flowers fill one terrace, vegetables another, grape vines another and so it goes all the way up the stairs. Once you're on S.W. Fairview Blvd., be sure to look across the street and up to your left. You can't miss Canterbury Castle.

Southwest Portland *Arlington Heights*

The ordinance against pouring boiling vats of oil over the parapets of Canterbury Castle is strictly enforced.

Southwest Portland *Arlington Heights*

Canterbury Castle

Canterbury Castle was built on speculation by J.O. Frye in 1930. With the Great Depression bearing down on the immediate world, it's no wonder that Frye was shy of a buyer. The property drew stares with its walls of uncoursed rock-faced stone and crenelated roof of uncut stone. Replete with a moat and drawbridge, Frye couldn't unload the property even when he attempted to rid himself of it through a raffle. The property was eventually sold in 1932.

Frye is also credited with designing and building the imaginative "Spider House" at 2997 Fairview Blvd. This particular theme home comes in the form of an English cottage with a mock thatched roof, eyelid dormers and a massive chimney of clinker brick. The round windows facing the street were made of leaded glass in a spider web pattern, hence the name.

Northeast Portland *Alameda-Beaumont*

Welcome to "The Alameda."

A real estate brochure from 1910 sings the praises of the Alameda Park development, "...commanding a magnificent view of the city and river and snow-covered mountains." Such is the truth in advertising. Both the Alameda and Beaumont neighborhoods sit comfortably on top of a northeast bluff that opens up to captivating views to the north, south, east and west. The desirable locale spawned extensive development from 1907 to 1929 and a wide array of architectural styles remain to this day. Quaint bungalows, stately Georgian brick homes and even a hacienda or two are all represented here. The namesake street, N.E. Alameda St., was originally called "The Alameda," and evoked images of gracious living up on the bluff. The "The" posed postal problems so the definite article was dropped after many years.

N.E. Alameda faithfully follows the bluff and in doing so, makes some erratic turns and tangles up into other streets. Stairs were a natural along the bluff to provide a direct route down the hill to trolleys, markets and commerce. The stairways built in the area between 1910 and 1912 have been determined to be of historically significance in the areas of transportation and landscape architecture.

The official Alameda neighborhood lies between N.E. 19th Ave. to the west and N.E. 33rd Ave. to the east, then N.E. Fremont St. to the south and N.E. Prescott St. to the north. The district of Beaumont begins south of N.E. Fremont St. at N.E. 33rd Ave. and continues east until about N.E. 57th Ave. On the south border, it's a bit unclear as to where Beaumont ends and the Hollywood district begins. No matter. Your main concern is to keep track of N.E. Alameda St. which is no simple task. The first set of stairs in the area starts on N.E. 19th Ave., right by Sabin Elementary School. The last stairway ends up all the way to N.E. 51st Ave. If you were to take in every staircase along the length of the bluff, you'd be logging 700-plus stairs.

Northeast Portland *Alameda-Beaumont*

N.E. Mason Street up to N.E. Crane Street
Year Built: 1975
Number of Stairs: 51
Top Locator: N.E. 19th Ave. and N.E. Crane Street
Bottom Locator: N.E. 19th Ave. and N.E. Mason Street
Thomas Guide: 596, J-1

Directions: From Pioneer Square (S.W. Yamhill St. and S.W. Broadway), take S.W. Yamhill St. east to S.W. 3rd Ave. Turn right on S.W. 3rd Ave. and turn left on S.W. Salmon St. Turn left on Naito Parkway and get in the left-turn lane for the Morrison Bridge. Take the Morrison Bridge over the river and follow signs to 99E. The off-ramp feeds you onto S.E. Belmont St. From S.E. Belmont St., turn left (north) on S.E. Grand Ave. Continue north on S.E. Grand Ave. (turns into Martin Luther King, Jr. Blvd.) for about two miles to N.E. Fremont St. Turn right on N.E. Fremont St. Go up to N.E. 21st Ave. and turn left. Turn left again on N.E. Alameda St., then make a quick right on N.E. 19th Ave. The stairway is directly ahead at the end of sidewalk.

❦ This stairway is a little off the Alameda beaten path but it's in the general vicinity. This set of stairs sees much more action than other stairs in the area since the Sabin Elementary school kids use them for their weekday commute.

Northeast Portland *Alameda-Beaumont*

N.E. Stuart Drive down to N.E. Ridgewood Drive
Year Built: 1974
Number of Stairs: 70
Top Locator: Corner of N.E. Stuart Dr. And N.E. Alameda St.
Bottom Locator: N.E. Ridgewood Dr.
Thomas Guide: 596, J-2

Directions: From Pioneer Square (S.W. Yamhill St. and S.W. Broadway), take S.W. Yamhill St. east to S.W. 3rd Ave. and make a right. Turn left on S.W. Salmon St. and turn left Naito Parkway. Get in the left-turn lane for the Morrison Bridge. Take the Morrison Bridge over the river and follow signs to 99E. The off-ramp feeds you onto S.E. Belmont St. From S.E. Belmont St., turn left (north) onto S.E. Grand Ave. Continue north on S.E. Grand (turns into Martin Luther King, Jr. Blvd.) for about two miles to N.E. Fremont St. Turn right on N.E. Fremont. Go up to N.E. 21st Ave. and turn left. Turn right on N.E. Alameda St. Go along N.E. Alameda for just about three streets and you'll see the top of this stairway on the southwest side of N.E. Stuart Dr. Look for a telephone pole with a one-way sign on it; the opening to the stairway is right there.

❦ The neighboring gardens seem to have escaped their borders to grace this stairway. Oregon grape, bracken fern and heather meander, hydrangeas flop and a tall holly tree stands sentinel along these stairs.

Northeast Portland *Alameda-Beaumont*

The Alameda-Ridgewood Stairs

Northeast Portland *Alameda-Beaumont*

N.E. Alameda Street down to N.E. Ridgewood Drive
Year Built: 1912
Number of Stairs: 70
Top Locator: 2644 N.E. Alameda St.
Bottom Locator: N.E. Ridgewood Dr.
Thomas Guide: 596, J-2

Directions: From Pioneer Square (S.W. Yamhill St. and S.W. Broadway), take S.W. Yamhill St. east to S.W. 3rd Ave. and make a right. Turn left on S.W. Salmon St. and turn left Naito Parkway. Get in the left-turn lane for the Morrison Bridge. Take the Morrison Bridge over the river and follow signs to 99E. The off-ramp feeds you onto S.E. Belmont St. From S.E. Belmont St., turn left (north) onto S.E. Grand Ave. Continue north on S.E. Grand (turns into Martin Luther King, Jr. Blvd.) for about two miles to N.E. Fremont St. Turn right on N.E. Fremont. Go up to N.E. 21st Ave. and turn left. Turn right on N.E. Alameda St. Go along N.E. Alameda just past S.E. Stuart Dr. The stairs begin next to the 2644 N.E. Alameda address.

❦ Built in 1912, this Alameda Terrace stairway is considered historically significant in the area of landscape architecture and development. The "curvilinear cheek wall" at the base of the stairs is worthy of being considered front cover material. There is an elegance to the line of the concrete wall that dresses up the whole stairway.

❦ The plant life along this stairway here is also worthy of notice. In addition to firethorn and St. John's wort, a massive, neighboring rock garden is in full view. Judging from the maturity of the garden, it could have been planted over 50 years ago. The broad range of ground cover, plants and shrubs continues to thrive on the steep hillside. Candytuft, bergenia and basket-of-gold spill over rocks and stealthy ajuga has crept out-of-bounds to carpet the risers of some stairs.

Northeast Portland *Alameda-Beaumont*

N.E. Alameda Terrace down to N.E. Fremont Street
Year Built: 1912
Number of Stairs: 88
Top Locator: 3130 N.E. Alameda Ter.
Bottom Locator: 3011 N.E. Fremont St.
Thomas Guide: 597, A-2

Directions: From Pioneer Square (S.W. Yamhill St. and S.W. Broadway), take S.W. Yamhill St. east to S.W. 3rd Ave. and make a right. Turn left on S.W. Salmon St. and turn left Naito Parkway. Get in the left-turn lane for the Morrison Bridge. Take the Morrison Bridge over the river and follow signs to 99E. The off-ramp feeds you onto S.E. Belmont St. From S.E. Belmont St., turn left (north) onto S.E. Grand Ave. Continue north on S.E. Grand (turns into Martin Luther King, Jr. Blvd.) for about two miles to N.E. Fremont St. Turn right on N.E. Fremont. Go up to N.E. 21st Ave. and turn left. Turn right on N.E. Alameda St. Continue along N.E. Alameda for several streets until you reach the intersection of N.E. 29th Ave. and N.E. Regents Dr. Just past this intersection, to the right, is N.E. Alameda Ter. Turn right onto N.E. Alameda Ter. The stairway begins next to the 3130 address.

❦ A big, beautiful birch marks the top of these stairs. The stairs themselves zigzag down the hill, looking like they fell out of a Paul Klee painting. Rhododendrons share the hill with bamboo and violets win their way through the cracks of a rock. Lights along the stairway are a welcome amenity during evening walks.

Northeast Portland *Alameda-Beaumont*

N. E. Alameda Terrace down to N.E. Fremont Street
Year Built: 1912
Number of Stairs: 65
Top Locator: 3250 N.E. Alameda Ter.
Bottom Locator: Intersection of N.E. 32nd Ave. and N.E. Fremont St.
Thomas Guide: 597, A-2

Directions: From Pioneer Square (S.W. Yamhill St. and S.W. Broadway), take S.W. Yamhill St. east to S.W. 3rd Ave. and make a right. Turn left on S.W. Salmon St. and turn left Naito Parkway. Get in the left-turn lane for the Morrison Bridge. Take the Morrison Bridge over the river and follow signs to 99E. The off-ramp feeds you onto S.E. Belmont St. From S.E. Belmont St., turn left (north) onto S.E. Grand Ave. Continue north on S.E. Grand (turns into Martin Luther King, Jr. Blvd.) for about two miles to N.E. Fremont St. Turn right on N.E. Fremont. Go up to N.E. 21st and turn left. Turn right on N.E. Alameda St. Continue along N.E. Alameda for several streets until you reach the intersection of N.E. 29th Ave. and N.E. Regents Dr. Just past the intersection, to the right, is N.E. Alameda Ter. Turn right onto N.E. Alameda Ter. The top of this stairway begins just before the street curves to join back up with N.E. Alameda St. Look for the 3250 N.E. Alameda Ter. address.

❦ Seas of ivy and a long juniper hedge dominate most of the hillside along this stairway. Bushels of berries on the cotoneaster catch the eye and deliver striking color even in the dead of winter.

Northeast Portland *Alameda-Beaumont*

N.E. Alameda Street down to N.E. Wistaria Drive
Year Built: Around 1913
Number of Stairs: 77
Top Locator: 3868 N.E. Alameda St.
Bottom Locator: Corner of N.E. 38th Ave. and N.E. Wistaria Dr.

Directions: From Pioneer Square (S.W. Yamhill St. and S.W. Broadway), take S.W. Yamhill St. east to S.W. 3rd Ave. and make a right. Turn left on S.W. Salmon St. and turn left Naito Parkway. Get in the left-turn lane for the Morrison Bridge. Take the Morrison Bridge over the river and follow signs to 99E. The off-ramp feeds you onto S.E. Belmont St. From S.E. Belmont St., turn left (north) onto S.E. Grand Ave. Continue north on S.E. Grand (turns into Martin Luther King, Jr. Blvd.) for about two miles to N.E. Fremont St. Turn right on N.E. Fremont. Turn right on N.E. Alameda St. The stairs are a few blocks past N.E. Fremont. Look for the 3868 address.

❦ Welcome to the Beaumont neighborhood. When the area was first developed in 1910, the Beaumont (French translation: beautiful mountain) area was considered a subdivision of Alameda. The elevation hardly defines the makings of a mountain but developers of yore are allowed a little hyperbole.

❦ This stairway is squeezed between two beautiful, brick 20th century Georgian homes. From the sidewalk, there's a walkway to the bluff where you'll be treated to a fabulous view. The stairway itself is a meandering one — six risers down to a landing, then seven steps down to another and so on. You'll see a lovely cottage garden planted with lilies, daylilies and bearded iris. Towards the bottom of the stairs there's a fragrant lilac and a long row of rhododendrons.

Then there's the graffiti. Some stairs are just magnets for "tagging." It's nagging.

N.E. Beaumont Street down to N.E. Wistaria Drive
Year Built: Around 1912
Number of Stairs: 117
Top Locator: 4196 N.E. Beaumont St.
Bottom Locator: 4211 N.E. Wistaria Dr. (corner of N.E. 42nd St.)
Thomas Guide: 597, B-3

Directions: From Pioneer Square (S.W. Yamhill St. and S.W. Broadway), take S.W. Yamhill St. east to S.W. 3rd Ave. and make a right. Turn left on S.W. Salmon St. and turn left Naito Parkway. Get in the left-turn lane for the Morrison Bridge. Take the Morrison Bridge over the river and follow signs to 99E. The off-ramp feeds you onto S.E. Belmont St. From S.E. Belmont St., turn left (north) onto S.E. Grand Ave. Continue north on S.E. Grand (turns into Martin Luther King, Jr. Blvd.) for about two miles to N.E. Fremont St. Turn right on N.E. Fremont and turn right on N.E. Alameda St. Continue along N.E. Alameda. N.E. Beaumont St. will appear to the right and share a section of N.E. Alameda for a few blocks. Look for the 4196 address and the path to the stairway will be on the right side of the street.

❦ There's a long brick retaining wall lining the sidewalk that leads to the bluff and the stairs. On this steep descent you'll see an entire hedge of camellias. There's bamboo too, plus hens and chicks sedum. Yucca pops up at the base of the stairs.

The lawn in front of this 20th C. Georgian home is perfection itself.

Northeast Portland *Alameda-Beaumont*

N.E. Beaumont Street down to N.E. Wistaria Drive
Year Built: Around 1912
Number of Stairs: 100
Top Locator: 4420 N.E. Beaumont St.
Bottom Locator: 4211 N.E. Wistaria Dr. (corner of N.E. 42nd St.)
Thomas Guide: 597, B-3

Directions: From Pioneer Square (S.W. Yamhill St. and S.W. Broadway), take S.W. Yamhill St. east to S.W. 3rd Ave. and make a right. Turn left on S.W. Salmon St. and turn left Naito Parkway. Get in the left-turn lane for the Morrison Bridge. Take the Morrison Bridge over the river and follow signs to 99E. The off-ramp feeds you onto S.E. Belmont St. From S.E. Belmont St., turn left (north) onto S.E. Grand Ave. Continue north on S.E. Grand (turns into Martin Luther King, Jr. Blvd.) for about two miles to N.E. Fremont St. Turn right on N.E. Fremont. Turn right on N.E. Alameda St. Continue along N.E. Alameda for about a mile. Go another four blocks past the last stairway. This set of stairs begins just beyond the 4420 address.

This 20th century gothic home is a standout.

N.E. Wistaria Drive down to N.E. 49th Avenue
Year Built: 1964
Number of Stairs: 31
Top Locator: N.E. Wistaria Dr.
Bottom Locator: Corner of N.E. 49th Ave. and Lower Wistaria Dr.
Thomas Guide: 597, C-3

Directions: From Pioneer Square (S.W. Yamhill St. and S.W. Broadway), take S.W. Yamhill St. east to S.W. 3rd Ave. and make a right. Turn left on S.W. Salmon St. and turn left Naito Parkway. Get in the left-turn lane for the Morrison Bridge. Take the Morrison Bridge over the river and follow signs to 99E. The off-ramp feeds you onto S.E. Belmont St. From S.E. Belmont St., turn left (north) onto S.E. Grand Ave. Continue north on S.E. Grand (turns into Martin Luther King, Jr. Blvd.) for about two miles to N.E. Fremont St. Turn right on N.E. Fremont and turn right on N.E. Alameda St. Continue on N.E. Alameda and make a hard right on N.E. Wistaria Dr. The stairs are on the left side of the street.

❦ At this point, the stairs on "The Alameda" have been exhausted, but N.E. Wistaria takes up the slack. Finding the next set of three stairways can be thoroughly confusing if you're driving in and around this odd pocket of streets. Park somewhere around the intersection of N.E. Alameda St. and N.E. Wistaria Dr. and walk to the stairs from there. You'll be glad you did.

Northeast Portland *Alameda-Beaumont*

N.E. Lower Wistaria Drive to N.E. 50th Avenue Dead-end
Year Built: 1965
Number of Stairs: 46
Top Locator: 4936 N.E. Wistaria Dr.
Bottom Locator: N.E. 50th Ave. dead-end
Thomas Guide: 597, C-3

Directions: From Pioneer Square (S.W. Yamhill St. and S.W. Broadway), take S.W. Yamhill St. east to S.W. 3rd Ave. and make a right. Turn left on S.W. Salmon St. and turn left Naito Parkway. Get in the left-turn lane for the Morrison Bridge. Take the Morrison Bridge over the river and follow signs to 99E. The off-ramp feeds you onto S.E. Belmont St. From S.E. Belmont St., turn left (north) onto S.E. Grand Ave. Continue north on S.E. Grand (turns into Martin Luther King, Jr. Blvd.) for about two miles to N.E. Fremont St. Turn right on N.E. Fremont and then right on N.E. Alameda St. Take N.E. Alameda all the way to N.E. Wistaria Dr. Make a soft right on the street just below N.E. Wistaria. The stairs are on the right side of the street.

❦ Ein stein of bier is only a slurp away at the "Rheinlander Bier Stube" on Sandy Blvd. If you're incentive oriented, strap on your lederhosen and begin the bluff walk from the base of these stairs. Make a round trip of it and top the excursion off with a fat, juicy bratwurst.

Northeast Portland *Alameda-Beaumont*

N.E. Wistaria Drive down to N.E. 51st Avenue Dead-end
Year Built: 1912
Number of Stairs: 83
Top Locator: 5136 N.E. Wistaria Dr.
Bottom Locator: N.E. 51st Ave. dead-end
Thomas Guide: 597, C-3

Directions: From Pioneer Square (S.W. Yamhill St. and S.W. Broadway), take S.W. Yamhill St. east to S.W. 3rd Ave. and make a right. Turn left on S.W. Salmon St. and turn left Naito Parkway. Get in the left-turn lane for the Morrison Bridge. Take the Morrison Bridge over the river and follow signs to 99E. The off-ramp feeds you onto S.E. Belmont St. From S.E. Belmont St., turn left (north) onto S.E. Grand Ave. Continue north on S.E. Grand (turns into Martin Luther King, Jr. Blvd.) for about two miles to N.E. Fremont St. Turn right on N.E. Fremont and then right on N.E. Alameda St. Take N.E. Alameda all the way to N.E. Wistaria Dr. Follow N.E. Wistaria to the right or east. After passing a few houses, look for the top of the stairway next to 5136 N.E. Wistaria.

❦ This stairway may also be approached from N.E. Sandy Blvd. Just make a left onto N.E. 51st Ave. from N.E. Sandy Blvd. and follow the road as it dead-ends at the base of the stairs. This is the last staircase in the line and it's a doozy. From the stairs you'll see the "Prime Rib" beckoning you in for a slab of beef. In 1931, this longtime Portland eatery was called "The Coon Chicken Inn."

Southeast Portland *Mt. Tabor*

Parking, volcano, picnic, playground....VOLCANO?

Mt. Tabor Park

Southeast Portland *Mt. Tabor*

Mt. Tabor is yet another example of the richness and variety of Portland's parks. The natural, wooded setting of Mt. Tabor lends itself to all types of activities from biking, hiking, picnicking, lazing about or...climbing stairs. In fact, Mt. Tabor is home to the true grand-daddy of all public stairways, boasting 287 risers divided into 15 flights. Though the climb is a steady uphill effort, the view from the top is worth any amount of exertion. The Portland skyline and the view of the west hills is nothing short of sublime.

As you wander through Mt. Tabor Park, you'll come across quite a few other stairways. Some will lead you from one reservoir to the next. Others simply offer the most direct route from the road up to a hillside hiking trail.

And let's not forget that Mt. Tabor is home to a volcano. It's completely inactive and has been so for many a millennium. But no other city in the country can claim such a distinction about an extinction. There aren't any stairs to speak of in or around the cinder cone but if you're mood for a quick geology lesson, it's the place to be.

There's also a story about the naming of Mt. Tabor. Portland pioneer Plympton Kelly had been reading *Napoleon and His Marshals* and was captivated by a French-Moslem battle that took place in the shadow of Mount Tabor in Palestine. Kelly was inspired to name the hill near his own homestead after this Palestinian peak.

Southeast Portland *Mt. Tabor*

S.E. 60th Avenue up to Mt. Tabor Reservoir #6
Year Built: 1911
Number of Stairs: 43
Top Locator: Reservoir #6
Bottom Locator: S.E. 60th Ave. and S.E. Hawthorne Blvd.
Thomas Guide: 597, D-7

Directions: From Pioneer Square (S.W. Broadway and S.W. Yamhill St.), take S.W. Yamhill St. east to S.W. 3rd Ave. and make a right. Then turn left on S.W. Salmon St. Turn left on Naito Parkway and get in the left-turn lane to approach the Morrison Bridge. Cross the Morrison Bridge and follow the signs to S.E. Belmont St. Stay on S.E. Belmont St. due east for about 2 -1/2 miles. At S.E. 39th Ave., you have to make a slight jog. Turn right on S.E. 39th Ave, then left on S.E. Yamhill St. and a quick left onto S.E. 40th Ave. At S.E. Belmont St., make a right and continue ahead. Turn right on S.E. 60th Ave. The stairs are across the intersection of S.E. Hawthorne Blvd. and S.E. 60th Ave.

❦ The narrowness of S.E. 60th Ave. has prompted residents along the west side of the street to park their cars on the sidewalk. Unless you've earned a special dispensation from the parking authorities, it's best to park on a side street like S.E. Main St.

❦ This stairway takes you up to Mt. Tabor's largest reservoir, inauspiciously named "Reservoir #6." Built in 1911, this reservoir holds 49 million gallons of water that originate in the Bull Run reservoir water system. Almost the size of a football field, Reservoir #6 is popular among walkers and joggers engaging in their constitutional. Seagulls seem to be at home in the reservoir, come rain or shine.

❦ The gate house on the corner of S.E. 60th Ave. and S.E. Division St. was saved from the demolition of Reservoir #2. Built in 1894, the oval pump house is made of cast stone and features rounded-arched windows.

Southeast Portland *Mt. Tabor*

Mt. Tabor Reservoir #6 to Reservoir #5
Year Built: 1911
Number of Stairs: 197
Top Locator: West side of Reservoir #5
Bottom Locator: East side of Reservoir #6
Thomas Guide: 597, D-7

Directions: From Pioneer Square (S.W. Broadway and S.W. Yamhill St.), take S.W. Yamhill St. east to S.W. 3rd Ave. and make a right. Then turn left on S.W. Salmon St. Turn left on Naito Parkway and get in the left-turn lane to approach the Morrison Bridge. Cross the Morrison Bridge and follow the signs to S.E. Belmont St. Stay on S.E. Belmont St. due east for about 2 -1/2 miles. At S.E. 39th Ave., you have to make a slight jog. Turn right on S.E. 39th Ave, then left on S.E. Yamhill St. and a quick left onto S.E. 40th Ave. At S.E. Belmont St., make a right and continue ahead. Turn right on S.E. 60th Ave. The stairs are on the east side of Reservoir #6.

❦ With nonexistent parking on S.E. 60th Ave., park on S.E. Main St., just north of Reservoir #6. You have to walk half way around Reservoir #6 and the stairs will start up, heading due east.

❦ These stairs are not only steep; they're awfully narrow as well. Take care and hang on to that railing. This first flight of 102 risers leads you up to a short walkway and a couple of short sets of stairs. The next flight of 90 stairs takes you up to the reservoir. There are fantastic views due west but focus on your feet until you reach the top of the stairs.

It's a long, steep climb to Reservoir #5.

Southeast Portland *Mt. Tabor*

Reservoir Loop Drive up to Hiking Trail
Year Built: Unknown
Number of Stairs: 31
Top locator: Hiking trail
Bottom Locator: Reservoir Loop Dr.
Thomas Guide: 597. E-7

Directions: From Pioneer Square (S.W. Broadway and S.W. Yamhill St.), take S.W. Yamhill St. east to S.W. 3rd Ave. and make a right. Then turn left on S.W. Salmon St. Turn left on Naito Parkway and get in the left-turn lane to approach the Morrison Bridge. Cross the Morrison Bridge and follow the signs to S.E. Belmont St. Stay on S.E. Belmont St. due east for about 2 -1/2 miles. At S.E. 39th Ave., you have to make a slight jog. Turn right on S.E. 39th Ave, then left on S.E. Yamhill St. and a quick left onto S.E. 40th Ave. At S.E. Belmont St., make a right and continue ahead. Make a right at S.E. 69th Ave. and follow the street around to the right and up into the park. The street at this entrance becomes Reservoir Loop Dr. and the railroad tie stairs begin up the hill, just off the road.

❦ Pat Billings, facilities and maintenance supervisor for the Mt. Tabor Park District, says that the wide variety of recreational activities on Mt. Tabor sometimes leads to conflicts among the various factions. Dog walkers don't much like eating a mountain biker's dust. Mountain bikers want to scream down a hillside path without the threat of an unleashed dog crossing their path. Joggers and others have their own gripes. Signs to designate appropriate path use have been discussed but more signs mean more graffiti. In an effort to make everyone happy, it's been bandied about that a sign saying "Don't Be Stupid" would cover all the bases.

Southeast Portland *Mt. Tabor*

Salmon Way up to Reservoir #1
Year Built: Unknown
Number of Stairs: 80
Top Locator: Reservoir #1
Bottom Locator: Salmon Wy.
Thomas Guide: 597, E-7

Directions: From Pioneer Square (S.W. Broadway and S.W. Yamhill St.), take S.W. Yamhill St. east to S.W. 3rd Ave. and make a right. Then turn left on S.W. Salmon St. Turn left on Naito Parkway and get in the left-turn lane to approach the Morrison Bridge. Cross the Morrison Bridge and follow the signs to S.E. Belmont St. Stay on S.E. Belmont St. due east for about 2 -1/2 miles. At S.E. 39th Ave., you have to make a slight jog. Turn right on S.E. 39th Ave, then left on S.E. Yamhill St. and a quick left onto S.E. 40th Ave. At S.E. Belmont St., make a right and continue ahead. Make a right at S.E. 60th Ave. and then a left on S.E. Stephens St. Turn right on Salmon Way. Continue down the road and you'll see the stairs to Reservoir #1 on the left, going up the hill.

❦ If you want to get away from the park hubbub, walking around the south side of the park is the way to do it. This side of Mt. Tabor is much more isolated and you can pick up some great hiking trails that will take you up to the summit, otherwise known as Harvey Scott Circle. A stern-looking statue of the man himself, Harvey Scott, sits on the summit's south side. With an outstretched arm pointing to Portland, Harvey W. Scott is remembered as a "Pioneer, Editor, Publisher." As one of the early publishers of *The Oregonian*, it is thought that Scott used the newspaper to spread his arch-conservative views.

Southeast Portland *Mt. Tabor*

S.E. Belmont Street up to S.E. Yamhill Court
Year Built: 1964
Number of Stairs: 31
Top Locator: S.E Yamhill Ct.
Bottom Locator: S.E. 66th Ave. and S.E. Belmont St.
Thomas Guide: 597, E-6

Directions: From Pioneer Square (S.W. Broadway and S.W. Yamhill St.),
take S.W. Yamhill St. east to S.W. 3rd Ave. and make a right. Then turn left
on S.W. Salmon St. Turn left on Naito Parkway and get in the left-turn lane
to approach the Morrison Bridge. Cross the Morrison Bridge and follow the
signs to S.E. Belmont St. Stay on S.E. Belmont St. due east for about 2 -1/2
miles. At S.E. 39th Ave., you have to make a slight jog. Turn right on S.E.
39th Ave, then left on S.E. Yamhill St. and a quick left onto S.E. 40th Ave. At
S.E. Belmont St., make a right and continue ahead. Keep going up S.E.
Belmont St. and you'll see the stairs on the right side of the street, next to
the S.E. Belmont Ave. and S.E. 66th Ave. street sign.

❦ If your ultimate goal is to make it up to Mt. Tabor Park, cross S.E. Yamhill
Ct. after you've reached the top of the stairs and follow the gravel path
between the houses. The park is directly ahead. As for parking, there isn't
any along this section of S.E. Belmont St.

Southeast Portland *Mt. Tabor*

S.E. Belmont Street up to S.E. Yamhill Street
Year Built: Unknown
Number of Stairs: 21
Top locator: S.E. Yamhill St.
Bottom Locator: S.E. Belmont St. and S.E. 67th Ave.
Thomas Guide: 597, E-6

Directions: From Pioneer Square (S.W. Broadway and S.W. Yamhill St.), take S.W. Yamhill St. east to S.W. 3rd Ave. and make a right. Then turn left on S.W. Salmon St. Turn left on Naito Parkway and get in the left-turn lane to approach the Morrison Bridge. Cross the Morrison Bridge and follow the signs to S.E. Belmont St. Stay on S.E. Belmont St. due east for about 2 -1/2 miles. At S.E. 39th Ave., you have to make a slight jog. Turn right on S.E. 39th Ave, then left on S.E. Yamhill St. and a quick left onto S.E. 40th Ave. At S.E. Belmont St., make a right and continue ahead. Keep going up S.E. Belmont St. and you'll see the stairs on the right side of the street, just up from the Belmont Ave. and S.E. 66th Ave. stairs.

❦ You can also get up to Mt. Tabor Park from this stairway. At the top of the stairs, cross the street and continue straight ahead. Follow the unimproved road that is sandwiched between the houses. This road will take you up to the park.

Southeast Portland *Mt. Tabor*

The Belmont-Scott Stairs

Southeast Portland *Mt. Tabor*

S.E. Belmont Street up to S.E. Scott Drive
Year Built: 1990
Number of Stairs: 18
Top Locator: S.E. Scott Dr. dead-end
Bottom Locator: North side of S.E. Belmont St. and S.E. 67th Ave.
Thomas Guide: 597, E-6

Directions: From Pioneer Square (S.W. Broadway and S.W. Yamhill St.), take S.W. Yamhill St. east to S.W. 3rd Ave. and make a right. Then turn left on S.W. Salmon St. Turn left on Naito Parkway and get in the left-turn lane to approach the Morrison Bridge. Cross the Morrison Bridge and follow the signs to S.E. Belmont St. Stay on S.E. Belmont St. due east for about 2 -1/2 miles. At S.E. 39th Ave., you have to make a slight jog. Turn right on S.E. 39th Ave, then left on S.E. Yamhill St. and a quick left onto S.E. 40th Ave. At S.E. Belmont St., make a right and continue ahead. There is no true intersection at S.E. 67th Ave. and Belmont St. but you'll see the street sign on the north or left side of the street. The #15 has a stop right at the base of the stairs.

❦ This S.E. Scott Dr. neighborhood is a gem with its lovely homes and well-tended gardens.

Rhododendron

Southeast Portland *Mt. Tabor*

The Grand-daddy of Portland stairs is in Mt. Tabor Park.

Southeast Portland *Mt. Tabor*

S.E. 69th Avenue up to Mt. Tabor Summit
Year Built: Unknown
Number of stairs: 287
Top Locator: Mt. Tabor Summit
Bottom Locator: Corner of S.E. 69th Ave. and S.E. Yamhill St.
Thomas Guide: 597, E-7

Directions: From Pioneer Square (S.W. Broadway and S.W. Yamhill St.), take S.W. Yamhill St. east to S.W. 3rd Ave. and make a right. Then turn left on S.W. Salmon St. Turn left on Naito Parkway and get in the left-turn lane to approach the Morrison Bridge. Cross the Morrison Bridge and follow the signs to S.E. Belmont St. Stay on S.E. Belmont St. due east for about 2 -1/2 miles. At S.E. 39th Ave., you have to make a slight jog. Turn right on S.E. 39th Ave, then left on S.E. Yamhill St. and a quick left onto S.E. 40th Ave. At S.E. Belmont St., make a right and continue ahead. Keep going up S.E. Belmont St. until it ends at S.E. 69th Ave. Turn right on S.E. 69th Ave. The entrance to the park and the stairs is directly ahead.

❧ This is the ultimate in Portland stairdom. Flight after flight after flight up to the summit, you'll breathlessly count a total of 287 stairs. The Mt. Tabor stairs are a challenge for all fitness levels, but you have to be in tip-top shape to run the entire length of these stairs. The stairway is long and steep and there are no stair sickness bags dispensed at the top.

❧ The fourth reservoir on Mt. Tabor is on this side of the park. It's actually a water tank covered by a large, flat disk that the locals refer to as the UFO landing pad.

Southeast Portland *Mt. Tabor*

S.E. 71st Avenue up to Mt. Tabor Park
Year Built: Unknown
Number of Stairs: 26
Top Locator: Mt. Tabor Park-Lower tennis courts
From Locator: Corner of S.E. 71st Ave. and S.E. Taylor St.
Thomas Guide: 597, E-7

Directions: From Pioneer Square (S.W. Broadway and S.W. Yamhill St.), take S.W. Yamhill St. east to S.W. 3rd Ave. and make a right. Then turn left on S.W. Salmon St. Turn left on Naito Parkway and get in the left-turn lane to approach the Morrison Bridge. Cross the Morrison Bridge and follow the signs to S.E. Belmont St. Stay on S.E. Belmont St. due east for about 2 -1/2 miles. At S.E. 39th Ave., you have to make a slight jog. Turn right on S.E. 39th Ave, then left on S.E. Yamhill St. and a quick left onto S.E. 40th Ave. At S.E. Belmont St., make a right and continue ahead. Keep going up S.E. Belmont St. until it runs into S.E. 69th Ave. Turn right on S.E. 69th Ave., left on S.E. Yamhill St. and right on S.E. 71st Ave. The stairs will be directly ahead, at the end of the block.

❦ This is a handy park entrance for local residents. The stairs take you from the street up to two tennis courts that are in need of a little sprucing up. Continue up the hill and you'll wander past towering evergreens. Eventually, you'll meet up with the Mt. Tabor stairs.

Southeast Portland *Mt. Tabor*

S.E. Thorburn Street down to S.E. Ash Avenue
Year Built: 1987
Number of Stairs: 56
Top Locator: 6505 S.E . Thorburn St.
Bottom Locator: 6502 S.E. Ash St.
Thomas Guide: 597, E-7

Directions: From Pioneer Square (S.W. Broadway and S.W. Yamhill St.), take S.W. Yamhill St. east to S.W. 3rd Ave. and make a right. Then turn left on S.W. Salmon St. Turn left on Naito Parkway and get in the left-turn lane to approach the Morrison Bridge. Cross the Morrison Bridge and follow the signs to S.E. Belmont St. Stay on S.E. Belmont St. due east for about 2 -1/2 miles. At S.E. 39th Ave., you have to make a slight jog. Turn right on S.E. 39th Ave, then left on S.E. Yamhill St. and a quick left onto S.E. 40th Ave. At S.E. Belmont St., make a right and continue ahead. Turn left on S.E. 60th Ave. and right on S.E. Thorburn St. The stairs are on the left side of the street not far past S.E. 63rd Ave.

❦ This stairway in the lovely Mt. Tabor neighborhood sits next to a colossal chalet on S.E. Thorburn St. Built in 1913, this large, dark brown residence gives off the charm of an Arts & Crafts style home with Swiss accents.

Southwest Portland *Southwest Hills*

The Elevator Stairs

It was an ongoing tradition in the Williams family to pile in the car and head out on a Portland adventure. Sometimes Dad would take us up to Lewis and Clark College. Other times we'd ramble along the railroad trestle on the way to the Old Pump House. Outings were never complete until we climbed the Elevator stairs. Hardly an adventure for some, but this very long staircase was a thrilling pilgrimage for all of us. For perched up on S.W. Hoffman was the apartment my parents lived in during their early years of marriage. We Williams kids were curiously drawn to this long, narrow apartment building.

Slowly scaling the stairs, we would plead with my father to give out details about the apartment, from the hardwood floors and the pot belly stove to where my sister Sarah slept when she was a baby. Dad patiently mapped out the newlywed nest and in doing so, conjured up a world of warmth, hope and happiness.

As we climbed higher and higher, I would become increasingly consumed by a disturbing notion; you had to climb this very long and very steep staircase every time, e-v-e-r-y single time, you went anywhere. What if you just wanted a loaf of bread down the grocery store? What about taking out the garbage? What if my Great Aunt Betty was to come for tea? The fact that S.W. Hoffman Rd. was quite serviceable for cars did not occur to me, such was my obsession with this matter.

The Editor relaxes on the "Elevator Stairs" before rubricating.

Southwest Portland *Southwest Hills*

S.W. Broadway Drive up to S.W. Hoffman Avenue
Year Built: Around 1937; Rebuilt 1984
Number of Stairs: 203
Top Locator: 2222 S.W. Hoffman Ave.
Bottom Locator: 2121 S.W. Broadway Dr.
Thomas Guide: 626, E-1

Directions: From Pioneer Square (S.W. Broadway and S.W. Yamhill St.), go south on S.W. Broadway as it makes its way through downtown and past Portland State University. Follow the signs to S.W. Broadway and once you cross I-405, the road will turn up the hill. At the base of the hill is a white office building (2121 S.W. Broadway). The narrow wood stairway begins just south of the parking lot on the west side of the street. Parking is limited on S.W. Broadway but if you go up the road to the first street on the right, S.W. Hoffman, you can find parking and take the stairs down instead of up.

❦ These are well-traveled stairs and many is the time the Buster and I have had to yield to a serious stair-stepper. I take it in stride when the merry little coeds breeze by, plowing up the stairs, two at a time. It's when the grand-pas-of-steel scream by that I pretend to have a keen interest in the sword ferns that abound on the hill.

❦ Listed in the Historic Resource Directory, this staircase was built in 1937 as a practical pedestrian alternative to driving up S.W. Broadway in hazardous winter conditions. In 1984, the City of Portland wanted to rebuild the stairway with steel to minimize maintenance. The neighborhood went up in arms, declaring that such an alteration of materials would harm the integrity of the stairway as a structure of historical significance. The new stairs are made of weather-treated wood and provide the perfect compromise.

❦ S.W. Hoffman was originally spelled Hoffmann. I'm sure there's a Tale here.

Southwest Portland *Southwest Hills*

The Old Reservoir Gate House
S.W. Cardinell-S.W. 10th Ave. Stairs

Southwest Portland *Southwest Hills*

S.W. Cardinell Drive down to S.W. 10th Avenue
Year Built: 1988
Number of Stairs: 55
Top Locator: 1249 S.W. Cardinell Dr.
Bottom Locator: 2066 S.W. 10th St.
Thomas Guide: 596, D-7

Directions: From Pioneer Square (S.W. Broadway and S.W. Yamhill St.), take S.W. Broadway south to S.W. Clay St. and make a right. At S.W. 13th Ave. turn left and stay in the left lane to S.W. Market St. Make a left on S.W. Market St., then a quick right on S.W. 12th Ave.; it's the only section of S.W. 12th Ave. that's two-way. You'll cross over I-405 and S.W. Cardinell Dr. will start up to your left. The stairs down to S.W. 10th Ave. begin on the left or east side of the street, just as S.W. Cardinell Dr. turns up to the right.

❦ If you're walking from the top of the S.W. Hoffman stairs, turn to the right and look for the "Starridge" sign. Just beyond the sign, a bike path begins. The path is surrounded by mounds of blackberry bushes until it empties out onto a residential development. Take the street down the hill, past the homes and to the gate. These stairs are to the right, just past the gate. The gate is a private entrance to the street but pedestrians may come and go as they please.

❦ The old Reservoir Gate House sitting firmly at the bottom of the stairs was built around 1890 and is one of Portland's oldest reservoirs. Fed by a small stream that ran down the hill slope, the reservoir collected the water and then routed it back up the hill for the residents up in Portland Heights. The reservoir was eventually abandoned due to the consistent shortage of water.

Southwest Portland *Southwest Hills*

Now presenting Willamette Week's 1994 "Best Stairway" — The Cardinell Stairs

Southwest Portland *Southwest Hills*

S.W. Cardinell Drive up to S.W. Cardinell Drive
Year Built: 1926
Number of Stairs: 160
Top Locator: 1295 S.W. Cardinell Dr.
Bottom Locator: 1209 S.W. Cardinell Dr.
Thomas Guide: 596, D-7

Directions: From Pioneer Square (S.W. Broadway and S.W. Yamhill St.), take S.W. Broadway south to S.W. Clay St. and make a right. Turn left on S.W. 13th Ave. and stay in the left lane. You'll run into S.W. Market St. Make a left, then a quick right on S.W. 12th Ave. It's only the two-way section of S.W. 12th Ave. Once you cross over I-405, the S.W. Cardinell stairs will start to the right of the 1209 S.W. Cardinell Drive house.

❦ *Willamette Week* spotlighted these 160 risers in their 1994 "Best of Portland" issue. It turns out that "The Best Stairway" submission was the whim of a staffer who simply took a liking to the stairs. While the research to find the ultimate stairway wasn't what you'd call empirically exhaustive, these stairs easily make the top 10.

❦ Dr. Y.T. Lam was the longtime resident of the "international" style house at the base of the stairs. Built in 1933, the home's unique amenities — an elevator and penthouse balcony — pale in comparison to Lam's own story. In 1914 at the age of 21, Yeuk T. Lam came to Portland from China to study medicine. The language barrier thwarted Lam's progress, and yet, he still managed to graduate from Ainsworth Elementary School in three years. Lam eventually went on to college and even to the University of Oregon Medical School. But it was the racism barrier that proved insurmountable. Lam was exposed as an "alien" and asked to leave medical school. Lam's alien status followed him to a Denver medical school and finally the AMA lowered the boom, declaring the Lam would never earn an American medical license. Lam turned his energies to naturopathic studies, passed his boards and he and his wife ran a very successful practice in Portland for about 50 years.

Southwest Portland *Southwest Hills*

The Hall-College Stairs

Southwest Portland *Southwest Hills*

S.W. Hall Street up to S.W. College Street
Year Built: 1981
Number of Stairs: 69
Top Locator: 1319 S.W. College St.
Bottom Locator: S.W. Hall St. dead-end
Thomas Guide: 626, D-7

Directions: From Pioneer Square (S.W. Broadway and S.W. Yamhill St.),
take S.W. Broadway south to S.W. Clay St. and make a right. Make a left on
S.W. 13th Ave. and stay in the left lane. You'll run into S.W. Market St. Make
a left then a quick right on S.W. 12th Ave. It's the only two-way section of
S.W. 12th Ave. You'll cross over I-405 and S.W. College St. will be on the
right. It's best to park here and walk down the lower section of S.W. College
St. The stairs will be on the right side of the street.

❦ S.W. College is a quirky, narrow street that connects up with S.W. Hall St.
and S.W. Upper Hall St. to make a hilly loop. These concrete stairs will take
you down to a neat row of townhouses that crop up at the end of the street.
If you follow S.W. Hall around the corner, you can take the proceeding stairs
and go back up to S.W. College St.

❦ There are several architecturally significant houses along S.W. College St.
Some have seen better days, others have been lovingly renovated. At 1225
S.W. College St., you'll find a Queen Anne Vernacular-style home built in
1880. According to the Historic Resource Directory, the house was built by
some of the Italian workmen who helped to construct S.W. Broadway Dr.
and Portland Ave. The men were given the option of either accepting
property or taking passage back to Italy once they completed their work.
Portland was their choice.

Southwest Portland *Southwest Hills*

The Hall-College Stairs #2

Southwest Portland *Southwest Hills*

S.W. Hall Street up to S.W. College Street
Year Built: Unknown
Number of Stairs: 110
Top Locator: 1303 S.W. College St.
Bottom Locator: 1320 S.W. Hall St.
Thomas Guide: 596, D-7

Directions: From Pioneer Square (S.W. Broadway and S.W. Yamhill St.), take S.W. Broadway south to S.W. Clay St. and make a right. Make a left on S.W. 13th Ave. and this time stay in the right lane, following signs to the freeways. Go past the freeway ramp and veer to your right on S.W. Montgomery Dr. Make a quick left on S.W. 14th Ave. and you'll run right into S.W. Hall St. The aggregate concrete stairs on the west side of 1320 S.W. Hall will connect to a path of stairs on the right. These stairs are followed by a series of railroad ties and cobblestone stairs, then wood risers. Eventually, the succession of stairs takes you all the way up to S.W. College St.

❦ Maybe these stairs were clearly listed in the Dept. of Pedestrian Transportation log book but their whereabouts eluded me for two years. After all, the top of the stairs looks like a private residential entrance and the stairs at the bottom are cleverly disguised as an apartment entry. It's a terrific discovery, a great vertical romp, and you'll pass by some historic homes and rambling gardens.

❦ Built in 1910, the Arts & Crafts-style home just up the road from the stairs (1421-1433 S.W. Hall St.) was the home of a daring individual, Dr. Marie Equi (1872-1952). A medical doctor, Equi was involved in a host of radical causes of the time, including women's suffrage and birth control. Equi also fervently opposed World War I, denouncing it as "The Big Barbecue." She was arrested for her outspoken views and not even her attorney, the great C.E.S. Wood, could overturn the verdict of sedition under the Espionage Act. Equi was shipped off to San Quentin where she spent a year and 10 months in prison before being pardoned.

Southwest Portland *Portland Heights*

"First you zig, then you zag."
Market-20th Stairs

Southwest Portland *Portland Heights*

S.W. 20th Avenue up to S.W. Market Street
Year Built: 1996
Number of Stairs: 82
Top Locator: 1950 S.W. Market St.
Bottom Locator: S.W. 20th Ave. dead-end
Thomas Guide: 596, D-6

Directions: From Pioneer Square (S.W. Broadway and S.W. Yamhill St.), take S.W. Broadway south to S.W. Jefferson St. and make a right. Continue on S.W. Jefferson St. over the I-405 overpass. Just after you go past the new light rail stop, make a left onto S.W. 20th Ave. The stairs begin right at the base of the dead-end street.

❦ The concrete is just now drying on this set of stairs that leads up to the monstrous white condominiums on S.W. Market St. While these condominiums are fabulously incongruous with the hillside architecture, there is hope that landscaping and balcony gardens will break up the linear, jarring bleakness with which we're currently confronted.

Southwest Portland *Portland Heights*

The Market-Vista Stairs

Southwest Portland *Portland Heights*

S.W. Market Street up to S.W. Vista Avenue
Year Built: 1929 (Vista to Mill); 1958 (Mill to Market)
Number of Stairs: 259
Top Locator: 1636 S.W. Vista Ave.
Bottom Locator: 1917 S.W. Market St.
Thomas Guide: 596, D-6

Directions: From Pioneer Square (S.W. Broadway and S.W. Yamhill St.),
take S.W. Broadway south to S.W. Jefferson St. and turn right. Make a left on
S.W. 14th Ave. (two-way street here), just over the I-405 overpass. This street
will turn into S.W. Market St. As you pass S.W. 19th Ave., look for 1917 S.W.
Market St. The stairway begins right across the street.

❦ This is one of my all-time favorite stairways, albeit tricky to find. The first
leg of the journey empties out onto S.W. Mill St. To your right, you'll see a
small gate guarding more steps. The sign on the gate states something to
the effect that this is private property but you may pass through if you don't
mess with our stuff. The original section of stairs here had ankle-wrenching
potential, so these replacement stairs are a dramatic improvement. Flowers
of thanks should be left on the homeowner's doorstep every time you pass.
Just don't pick the posies from their garden.

❦ The Market Street-Vista staircase sparked the idea for this book. In 1989, I
was living up in Portland Heights and working downtown at Jake's Catering.
As walking is my transportation of choice, I scouted out the most direct
route from Point A to Point B. It turned out that this staircase offered a
straight shot down the hill, saving me scads of time. The morning amble
down and the nightly heave-ho up prompted much contemplation — the
beauty of the city, Mt. Hood in the distance, the ever lovin' cramp in my
thigh. I relished the commute and I'm thoroughly convinced that this
staircase saved me from certain blimpage brought on by Jake's flourless
chocolate cake; a food stuff I quietly consumed throughout each work day.

Southwest Portland *Portland Heights*

Vista-Prospect Stairs

Southwest Portland *Portland Heights*

S.W. Vista Avenue up to S.W. Prospect Drive
Year Built: 1957
Number of Stairs: 13 stairs
Top Locator: 1725 S.W. Prospect Dr.
Bottom Locator: 1456 S.W. Vista Ave.
Thomas Guide: 596, D-6

Directions: From Pioneer Square (S.W. Broadway and S.W. Yamhill St.), take S.W. Broadway south to S.W. Taylor St. and turn right or west. At S.W. 17th Ave., make a left, then a quick right onto S.W. Salmon St. (two-way street here). Go up the hill past the Multnomah Athletic Club. The road takes a little jog at S.W. King Ave. where it turns into S.W. Park Pl. Two streets past the S.W. King Ave. intersection, make a left on S.W. Vista Ave. The stairs are to the south of Vista Bridge, on the right side of the street, next to the 20mph speed caution sign.

❦ Parking is impossible along this stretch of S.W. Vista Ave. so it's best to park on a side street, like S.W. Madison St. From S.W. Madison St. you can walk to S.W. Vista Ave., cross Vista Bridge and continue up the street to the stairs. There are also two "connect the cases" options. From the top of the Market-Vista stairs, turn right on S.W. Vista Ave. and the stairs are just down the hill on your left. From the top of the Market-20th stairs, turn right on S.W. Market St. and walk up to S.W. Vista Ave. Turn left on S.W. Vista Ave. and the stairs are just up the street on the right.

❦ This stair-path combo is a real find and great shortcut up to S.W. Prospect Dr. The three stubby stairs on S.W. Vista take you up to a path between two chain link fences. This path runs between two huge houses, then ends with a set of 10 stairs. Once you're up on S.W. Prospect Dr., you'll be confronted by a conifer of great girth shooting up to the sky.

Southwest Portland *Portland Heights*

*Portland Heights
circa 1915*

Southwest Portland *Portland Heights*

S.W. Montgomery Drive up to S.W. Vista Avenue
Year Built: 1910
Number of Stairs: 40
Top Locator: S.W. Vista Ave.
Bottom Locator: 1698 S.W. Montgomery Dr.
Thomas Guide: 596, D-6

Directions: From Pioneer Square (S.W. Broadway and S.W. Yamhill St.), take S.W. Broadway south to S.W. Taylor St. and turn right or west. At S.W. 17th Ave., make a left, then a quick right onto S.W. Salmon St. (two-way street here). Go up the hill past the Multnomah Athletic Club. The road takes a little jog at S.W. King Ave. where it turns into S.W. Park Pl. Two streets past the S.W. King Ave. intersection, make a left on S.W. Vista Ave. and head up the hill. The stairs are found on the left side of S.W. Vista Ave., just past where S.W. Montgomery comes up the east side of the hill.

❦ These stairs are leftovers from the trolley times. They still come in handy is you want to quickly drop down to S.W. Montgomery Dr.

Southwest Portland *Portland Heights*

St. Helens Court Footbridge

Southwest Portland *Portland Heights*

S.W. Saint Helens Court up to S.W. Vista Avenue
Year Built: Unknown
Number of Stairs: 62
Top Locator: S.W. Vista Ave.
Bottom Locator: 2526 S.W. Saint Helens Ct.
Thomas Guide: 596, C-7

Directions: From Pioneer Square (S.W. Broadway and S.W. Yamhill St.), take S.W. Broadway south to S.W. Taylor St. and turn right or west. At S.W. 17th Ave., make a left, then a quick right onto S.W. Salmon St. (two-way street here). Go up the hill past the Multnomah Athletic Club. The road takes a little jog at S.W. King Ave. where it turns into S.W. Park Pl. Two streets past the S.W. King Ave. intersection, make a left on S.W. Vista Ave. and head up the hill. At the first traffic light, S.W. Elm St., make a right. Turn left onto S.W. Montgomery Dr., then a quick left onto S.W. Saint Helens Ct. Look for the 2526 address and you'll see the footbridge to the right. After crossing the footbridge, the next set of stairs is up to the right at the "Children Crossing" sign. Take the stairs up to the Ainsworth schoolyard. Cross the yard and there will be 24 more steps leading up to S.W. Vista Ave.

❦ If this is stretching the definition of a stairway, think of it as an urban orienteering exercise. The footbridge is a treat and the gravel path lined with footlights makes for a delightful evening walk.

An old footbridge neighbor, this 1923 Arts & Crafts-style home features a magnificent, massive roof and a unique octagonal-shaped window on the front door.

Southwest Portland *Portland Heights*

"Pen-y-bry"

Southwest Portland *Portland Heights*

S.W. Montgomery Drive up to S.W. Alta Vista Place
Year Built: Unknown
Number of Stairs: 40
Top Locator: 2633 S.W. Alta Vista Pl.
Bottom Locator: 2575 S.W. Montgomery Dr.
Thomas Guide: 596, C-7

Directions: From Pioneer Square (S.W. Broadway and S.W. Yamhill St.), take S.W. Broadway south to S.W. Taylor St. and turn right or west. At S.W. 17th Ave., make a left, then a quick right onto S.W. Salmon St. (two-way street here). Go up the hill past the Multnomah Athletic Club. The road takes a little jog at S.W. King Ave. and turns into S.W. Park Pl. Two streets past the S.W. King Ave. intersection, make a left on S.W. Vista Ave. and head up the hill. Turn right at the first traffic light, S.W. Elm St. The street is about a 1/2 mile from the Vista Bridge and right before Ainsworth Elementary School. Make a left onto S.W. Montgomery Dr., go up about an 1/8 of a mile. The opening to the staircase is cut into the high retaining wall.

❧ S.W. Alta Vista Pl. is a quaint, short street and home to some of the most beautiful residences and gardens in Portland. This is particularly true of the home at the end of the street, "Pen-y-bry." Welsh for "Crest of the Hill," this outstanding Arts & Crafts-style home was built in 1925 by Jack Edwards. At the time, Edwards' Hay Creek Ranch was the largest in Oregon and his largesse is tastefully evident in this home. Unique architectural features include the slate roof imported from Wales. The huge fireplace in the reception hall came from Edward's ancestral home in Wales.

Southwest Portland *Portland Heights*

"Stairs just for sitting."
Jewett Park Stairs

Southwest Portland *Portland Heights*

S.W. Spring Street up to S.W. Vista Avenue
Year Built: 1974
Number of Stairs: 18
Top Locator: S.W. Vista Ave.
Bottom Locator: Corner of S.W. Spring Ave. and S.W. Vista Ave.
Thomas Guide: 596, D-7

Directions: From Pioneer Square (S.W. Broadway and S.W. Yamhill St.), take S.W. Broadway south to S.W. Taylor St. and turn right or west. At S.W. 17th Ave., make a left, then a quick right onto S.W. Salmon St. (two-way street here). Go up the hill past the Multnomah Athletic Club. The road takes a little jog at S.W. King Ave. where it turns into S.W. Park Pl. Two streets past the S.W. King Ave. intersection, make a left on S.W. Vista Ave. and head up the hill until you see Ainsworth School on your right and Vista Spring Cafe on your left. The Jewett Park stairs are just south of Ainsworth, on the same side of the street.

❧ Portland is home to the nation's largest city park, Forest Park, and to the country's smallest park, Mill Ends Park. So it should come as no surprise to discover that our fair city is home to a stair park, Jewett Park. The graceful cascade of stairs was created by Mr. Bill Jewett and dedicated in honor of the Jewett family, a longtime Portland family. The side wall at the base of the stairs reveals a bronze plaque that bears the inscription, "There is nothing like sitting on steps in the sun when one has the unparalleled pleasure of doing just nothing at all."

Southwest Portland *Portland Heights*

The Elizabeth Street Stairs
circa 1895

Southwest Portland *Portland Heights*

S.W. Vista Avenue up to S.W. Elizabeth Street
Year Built: Around 1895 **Rebuilt:** 1966
Number of Stairs: 70
Top Locator: 2529 S.W. Elizabeth St.
Bottom Locator: Corner of S.W. Vista Ave. and S.W. Spring St.
Thomas Guide: 596, C-7

Directions: From Pioneer Square (S.W. Broadway and S.W. Yamhill St.), take S.W. Broadway south to S.W. Taylor St. and turn right or west. At S.W. 17th Ave., make a left, then a quick right onto S.W. Salmon St. (two-way street here). Go up the hill past the Multnomah Athletic Club. The road takes a little jog at S.W. King Ave. where it turns into S.W. Park Pl. Two streets past the S.W. King Ave. intersection, make a left on S.W. Vista Ave. and head up the hill to S.W. Spring St. On the southeast side or left side of S.W. Vista, just past the intersection, is the beginning of an elevated sidewalk. Follow the sidewalk for about 100 yards and the beginning of the stairs will be on your left.

❦ Built around 1895, this well-maintained staircase provides plenty of risers to get your heart pumping, plus it offers a strong pipe railing should you need assistance. Giant laurel bushes hover above you all along the stairway and the tiny, trim S.W. Elizabeth Street greets you at the top. According to the Historic Resource Inventory, this stairway was used by cable car commuters who would take the stairs to get to the "Tea House" up on S.W. Hawthorne Terrace. Horse-drawn carriages were also parked at the foot of the stairs while owners enjoyed a spot of tea up on the hill.

Southwest Portland *Portland Heights*

S.W. Broadway Drive up to S.W. Davenport Street
Year Built: 1929
Number of Stairs: 37
Top Locator: 1617 S.W. Davenport St.
Bottom Locator: Corner of S.W. Broadway Dr. and S.W. Davenport St.
Thomas Guide: 626, D-1

Directions: From Pioneer Square (S.W. Broadway and S.W. Yamhill St.), go south on S.W. Broadway as it makes its way through downtown and past Portland State University. Follow the signs to S.W. Broadway Dr. and once you cross I-405, take S.W. Broadway Dr. up the hill for about a mile. You'll see the base of the stairs right before you reach the intersection of S.W. Broadway Dr. and S.W. Davenport St. Parking is available on S.W. Davenport St.

❦ It's pretty crazy traffic-wise along this stretch of S.W. Broadway Dr., making these stairs a great escape. If you need to park, your best bet is up on S.W. Davenport St.

❦ Governors Park is just up the road on S.W. Davenport St. The Park was created in honor of Oregon Governor Sylvester Pennoyer who held the office for two terms from 1887 to 1898.

"S-l-o-w D-o-w-n!"

Southwest Portland *Portland Heights*

S.W. Broadway Drive up to S.W. Terrace Drive
Year Built: 1991
Number of Stairs: 59
Top Locator: S.W. Terrace Dr. dead-end
Bottom Locator: 1735 S.W. Broadway Dr.
Thomas Guide: 626, D-1

Directions: From Pioneer Square (S.W. Broadway and S.W. Yamhill St.), go south on S.W. Broadway as it makes its way through downtown and past Portland State University. Follow the signs to S.W. Broadway Dr. and once you cross I-405, take S.W. Broadway Dr. up the hill for about a mile. Keep a watch out for the 1735 address just past S.W. Davenport St. Parking is difficult on S.W. Broadway Dr. so your only option is a side street.

❦ This is a quiet unassuming staircase. It's a shady, pleasant ascent and offers great peeks into backyards and gardens.

Southwest Portland *Portland Heights*

Broadway-Gerald Stairs

Southwest Portland *Portland Heights*

S.W. Broadway Drive up to S.W. Gerald Avenue
Year Built: 1991
Number of Stairs: 42
Top Locator: 2662 S.W. Gerald Ave.
Bottom Locator: 2201 S.W. Broadway Dr.
Thomas Guide: 626, C-1

Directions: From Pioneer Square (S.W. Broadway and S.W. Yamhill St.), go south on S.W. Broadway as it makes its way through downtown and past Portland State University. Follow the signs to S.W. Broadway Dr. and once you cross I-405, the road will turn up the hill. Take S.W. Broadway Dr. up the hill for just over a mile. Watch out for the 2201 address. The stairs will be on your right. Again, with limited parking, the side streets are your best bet.

❦ This is another fine, quiet staircase, offering a shady sojourn up to S.W. Gerald Ave. If you want to loop over to the Broadway-Terrace staircase, make a right on S.W. Gerald Ave., then another right on S.W. Terrace Dr. and walk down to the end of the street. The stairs are on your left. There's also a new hiking trail right across from the base of the stairs on S.W. Broadway Dr. The trail is a subset of the 40-mile loop trail that runs through the southwest hills. From this point of departure you have several hiking options, ranging from going all the way up to Council Crest to making your way down to the Marquam Shelter.

Southwest Portland *Portland Heights*

S.W. Edgewood Road up to S.W. Edgewood Loop
Year Built: Around 1920
Number of Stairs: 23
Top Locator: 1831 S.W. Edgewood Rd.
Bottom Locator: S.W. Edgewood Rd. dead-end
Thomas Guide: 626, D-1

Directions: From Pioneer Square (S.W. Broadway and S.W. Yamhill St.), go south on S.W. Broadway as it makes its way through downtown and past Portland State University. Follow the signs to S.W. Broadway Dr. and once you cross I-405, take S.W. Broadway Dr. up the hill past S.W. Davenport St. S.W. Edgewood Rd. will be on your left. Make a hard left turn on S.W. Edgewood Rd. If you're driving, park now — this street is narrow. Walk to the street's end (about a 1/4 mile) and you'll find this secret stairway and dirt path which loops you back up to S.W. Edgewood Rd.

❧ S.W. Edgewood's width, 16-18 feet, was substandard even when the street was built in the 1920's. It was originally named Kline Street.

❧ The set of stairs at the end of the street isn't terribly long or historically significant but terribly secret and shady-dark — an enchanting discovery.

Southwest Portland *Portland Heights*

S.W. Broadway Drive up to S.W. Ravensview Drive
Year Built: Around 1920
Number of Stairs: 20
Top Locator: 2696 S.W. Ravensview Dr.
Bottom Locator: Corner of S.W. Broadway Dr. and S.W. Ravensview Dr.
Thomas Guide: 626, D-1

Directions: From Pioneer Square (S.W. Broadway and S.W. Yamhill St.), go south on S.W. Broadway as it makes its way through downtown and past Portland State University. Follow the sign to S.W. Broadway Dr. and once you cross I-405, take S.W. Broadway Dr. up the hill, past S.W. Davenport St. The next street you can make a right on is S.W. Ravensview Dr. The stairs are visible from the road but, if driving, you need to turn up S.W. Ravensview Dr. and park on the street.

❦ As is the case with the S.W. Davenport St. stairs and others along S.W. Broadway Dr., this S.W. Ravensview Dr. stairway access is related to the trolley system that ran up and around Portland Heights. While these stairs have a significant place in Portland history, they might be upstaged by a little something over on the adjacent street of S.W. Corona Ave. In the backyard of 2626 S.W. Corona Ave. is a gravestone of an early Native American. The Historic Resource Directory indicates that the gravestone is of archaeological significance but gives no further information.

Southwest Portland *Portland Heights*

"Short and Sweet" Arden-Sherwood Stairs

S.W. Arden Road down to S.W. Sherwood Drive
Year Built: 1987
Number of Stairs: 8
Top Locator: 2490 S.W. Arden Rd.
Bottom Locator: 2449 S.W. Sherwood Dr.
Thomas Guide: 626, C-1

Directions: From Pioneer Square (S.W. Broadway and S.W. Yamhill St.), go south on S.W. Broadway as it makes its way through downtown and past Portland State University. Follow the signs to S.W. Broadway Dr. and once you cross I-405, take S.W. Broadway Dr. up the hill, past S.W. Edgewood Dr. and S.W. Sherwood Dr. Make a left on S.W. Arden Rd. Look for the 2490 S.W. Arden Rd. address.

❦ This is one of the shortest sets of stairs cataloged in the book, but it measures up in my estimation. There's a pale pink concrete path that also serves as a driveway. The pink path turns to dirt as it feeds between some lovely backyards and ends up on S.W. Sherwood Dr. with a small exclamation of stairs.

Southwest Portland *Portland Heights*

"Fountain of Youth" — Patton-Talbot Stairs

S.W. Patton Road up to S.W. Talbot Road
Year Built: Unknown
Number of Stairs: 23 stairs
Top Locator: 2612 S.W. Talbot Rd.
Bottom Locator: Corner of S.W. Patton Rd. and S.W. Vista Ave.
Thomas Guide: 626, C-1

Directions: From Pioneer Square (S.W. Broadway and S.W. Yamhill St.), take S.W. Broadway south, past Portland State University. Follow the signs to S.W. Broadway Dr. and once you cross I-405, take S.W. Broadway Dr. up the hill. At the first stop sign, S.W. Broadway Dr. turns into S.W. Patton Rd. The stairs are to the left, just past the stop sign and behind the drinking fountain.

❦ Local lore has it that "The Fountain" was quite the hot spot in the early 60's for high school hooligans who now sport Dockers or own fishing lodges. The grassy slope alongside the stairs was the perfect perch for making an instant I.D. on friend, foe or parent that might be approaching "The Fountain." The green lawn has long since been since replaced by shrubbery, possibly as a deterrent to "teenaging." A stand of four big trees remains as does the water fountain, offering welcome refreshment for the stair trekker.

Southwest Portland *Portland Heights*

S.W. Greenway Avenue up to S.W. Summit Drive
Year Built: Unknown
Number of Stairs: 36
Top Locator: S.W. Summit Dr. dead-end
Bottom Locator: 2770 S.W. Greenway Ave.
Thomas Guide: 626, C-1

Directions: From Pioneer Square (S.W. Broadway and S.W. Yamhill St.), take S.W. Broadway south to S.W. Taylor St. and turn right or west. At S.W. 17th Ave., make a left, then a quick right onto S.W. Salmon St. (two-way street here). Go up the hill past the Multnomah Athletic Club. The road takes a little jog at S.W. King Ave. where it turns into S.W. Park Pl. Two streets past the S.W. King Ave. intersection, make a left on S.W. Vista Ave. and head all the way up the hill to the S.W. Patton Rd. intersection. Make a left on S.W. Patton Rd., and a quick left onto S.W. Greenway Ave. (second street past the intersection). Keep your eyes peeled to the addresses on the right side of the street. The 2770 S.W. Greenway Ave. address is well marked. Look straight across the street and you'll see the stairs.

Rhododendron

Southwest Portland *Portland Heights*

S.W. Greenway Avenue down to S.W. Montgomery Drive
Year Built: 1985
Number of Stairs: 70
Top Locator: 2851 S.W. Greenway Ave.
Bottom Locator: 2846 S.W. Montgomery Dr.
Thomas Guide: 626, C-1

Directions: From Pioneer Square (S.W. Broadway and S.W. Yamhill St.), take S.W. Broadway south to S.W. Taylor St. and turn right or west. At S.W. 17th Ave, make a left, then a quick right onto S.W. Salmon St. (two-way street here). Go up the hill past the Multnomah Athletic Club. The road takes a little jog at S.W. King Ave. where it turns into S.W. Park Pl. S.W. Vista Ave. is two streets past S.W. King Ave. Make a left on S.W. Vista Ave. and head up the hill to the S.W. Patton Rd. Turn right on S.W. Patton Rd., then make a quick left onto S.W. Greenway Ave. (second street past the intersection). The top of the stairs is on the right side of the street.

❦ The beginning of this wooden stairway masquerades as a private stairway. The first series of stairs leads to a steep dirt and gravel pathway shouldered by very tall hedges. Then comes a group of concrete stairs that takes you down to the street.

Hollyhock

Southwest Portland *Portland Heights*

S.W. Greenway Avenue down to S.W. Talbot Road
Year Built: Unknown
Number of Stairs: 22
Top Locator: Corner of S.W. Greenway Ave. and Talbot Rd.
Bottom Locator: Corner of S.W. Talbot Ter. and S.W. Fairmount Blvd.
Thomas Guide: 626, C-1

Directions: From Pioneer Square (S.W. Broadway and S.W. Yamhill St.), take S.W. Broadway south to S.W. Taylor St. and turn right or west. At S.W. 17th Ave., make a left, then a quick right onto S.W. Salmon St. (two-way street here). Go up the hill past the Multnomah Athletic Club. The road takes a little jog at S.W. King Ave. where it turns into S.W. Park Pl. S.W. Vista Ave. is two streets past S.W. King Ave. Make left on S.W. Vista Ave. and head all the way up the hill. Make a right on S.W. Patton Rd., then an immediate left onto S.W. Talbot Rd. Carefully follow the road around the bend and soon you'll see the Greenway viaduct directly ahead. Pass under the viaduct; you'll see the stairway on the left side.

❧ This set of stairs is key for creating a great three-stairway loop. At the top of the stairs, you'll be on S.W. Greenway Ave. Cross the street and take the S.W. Greenway Ave. boardwalk down the road to the right. Look for the opening of the previous stairway at 2851 S.W. Greenway Ave. and take the stairs down the hill. Once you're on S.W. Montgomery Dr., take a left and go up the hill to the next stairway located at 2944 S.W. Montgomery Dr. Take the stairs up the hill and you'll be back under the Greenway viaduct. To complete the loop, turn left and walk under the viaduct to the first set of stairs.

Talbot-Greenway Stairs

Southwest Portland *Portland Heights*

S.W. Talbot Road down to S.W. Montgomery Drive
Year Built: 1985
Number of Stairs: 47
Top Locator: Under the Greenway Viaduct
Bottom Locator: 2944 S.W. Montgomery
Thomas Guide: 626, C-1

Directions: From Pioneer Square (S.W. Broadway and S.W. Yamhill), take S.W. Broadway south to S.W. Taylor and turn right or west. At S.W. 17th, make a left, then a quick right onto S.W. Salmon (two-way street here). Go up the hill past the Multnomah Athletic Club. The road takes a little jog at S.W. King where it turns into S.W. Park. S.W. Vista is two streets past S.W. King Ave. Make left on S.W. Vista and head all the way up the hill. Make a right at S.W. Broadway-S.W. Patton Road, then an immediate left onto S.W. Talbot Road. Carefully follow the road around the bend and soon you'll see the Greenway viaduct directly ahead. The top of the stairs are on the left side of the street, right before you go under the viaduct.

☙ How can two staircases that originate in fairly close proximity end up on totally different streets? Like its neighbor, this stairway was built in 1985 but only wood was used in the construction. The stairs are separated by a foot path. Great garden viewing.

Southwest Portland *Portland Heights*

"Lonely at the Top"
Council Crest

Southwest Portland *Portland Heights*

S.W. Council Crest Court down to S.W. Hillsboro Avenue
Year Built: 1985
Number of Stairs: 47
Top Locator: 3547 S.W. Council Crest Ct
Bottom Locator: 2766 S.W. Hillsboro St.
Thomas Guide: 626, C-1

Directions: From Pioneer Square (S.W. Broadway and S.W. Yamhill St.), take S.W. Broadway south to S.W. Taylor St. and turn right or west. At S.W. 17th Ave., make a left, then a quick right onto S.W. Salmon St. (two-way street here). Go up the hill past the Multnomah Athletic Club. The road takes a little jog at S.W. King Ave. where it turns into S.W. Park Pl. Two streets past the S.W. King Ave. intersection, make a left on S.W. Vista and head up the hill. Make a right on S.W. Patton Rd. intersection and then a quick left on S.W. Greenway Ave. Follow S.W. Greenway Ave. up towards Council Crest Park. S.W. Greenway feeds into S.W. Council Crest Ct. The stairs are on the west side of S.W. Council Crest Ct.

❦ Council Crest Park has experienced some interesting transformations throughout its almost 100 years. The location was officially named in July of 1898. George H. Himes, then Oregon Historical Society curator, called a gathering of ministers to the site. "Council Crest" was mutually agreed upon because the Columbia River Indians had long used this hill for powwows.

❦ The peaceful, panoramic setting was soon to change after the Lewis & Clark Exposition of 1905. The land was purchased to build Council Crest Amusement Park. The Park opened with much fanfare in 1907, catering to the sensibilities of the time — a scenic railroad, a dance hall and the Tunnel of Love (Admission 10 cents). The Great Depression took its toll on the rollicking fun and the Park closed down in 1929. By 1933, all that was left of Council Crest Park was a labyrinth of broken down gates and boarded up buildings. Council Crest Park has somewhat returned to its bucolic beginnings and continues to be a big draw among tourists, hikers and folks who still long for The Tunnel of Love.

Southwest Portland *Portland Heights*

Fairmount-Chesapeake Stairs

Southwest Portland *Portland Heights*

S.W. Fairmount Boulevard down to S.W. Chesapeake Avenue
Year Built: 1985
Number of Stairs: 68
Top Locator: S.W. Wapato and S.W. Fairmount Blvd.
Bottom Locator: 4089 S.W. Chesapeake
Thomas Guide: 626, C-2

Directions: From downtown S.W. Broadway and S.W. Yamhill, take S.W. Broadway south, through the city and up into the southwest hills. Just past the intersection of S.W. Broadway, S.W. Vista and S.W. Patton Rd., you'll see S.W. Greenway on your left. Turn left onto S.W. Greenway and you'll turn right onto S.W. Fairmount, heading due south. Follow S.W. Fairmount for about 6/10 of a mile and look to your left for the S.W. Wapato street sign. The stairs begin on the right or south side of the street.

❦ Fairmount Blvd. is a popular three-mile loop frequented by joggers, walkers, cyclists, baby strollers and dogs. This hilltop route is appealing because it's fairly simple to get to, the grade is relatively flat and, depending on the weather and time of day, the views to the west are stunning. The architectural styles of homes are varied but many share a familiar stilt construction that surely defies the laws of gravity. The 1996 flood has taken its toll along the route and mud slides have left gouges in the hillside above the street. The Chesapeake stairs off of Fairmount are a convenient addition for lower hillside residents or for those wishing to add stair drills to a workout routine. The stairs themselves only go part of the way down the hill and then a gravel trail takes you down to the S.W. Chesapeake Avenue. This street was built around 1905 and nicknamed "The Goat Trail" by the neighborhood. The reference has nothing to do with livestock but rather to the steepness of the road, an incline accessible only to goats or other cloven-footed beasts.

Northwest Portland *Alphabet District*

The Summit-Westover Stairs

Northwest Portland *Alphabet District*

The Northwest Hills

It's always an adventure to go from the mole hills to the foothills to the top of the hilly hills of Northwest Portland. This is especially true if you incorporate any number of public stairways that spring up in the area. Northwest Portland is not just serious stair-stepping territory, it's heavy historic territory. Eleven out of 12 stairways have been recognized as historically significant in the Oregon Resource Directory. There are also many homes in the Kings Heights and Westover Terrace neighborhoods that are either architecturally distinct, were owned by someone of distinction or can claim that Hemingway distinctly slept there (2665 N.W. Cornell Road).

Kings Heights and Westover Terraces were platted just after 1909. Developers were hopeful to see a similar return on investment as witnessed all over Portland Heights. The recession of 1914 did little to encourage growth and the lack of a reliable streetcar system in the area didn't help matters either. It wasn't until the 1920's that upwardly mobile Portlanders were again able to exercise the old adage — the better the view, the richer the viewer. Just ask Mr. Pittock. The wealthy came. They built. They expanded.

There are several stairways that start up from the Alphabet streets in the flatlands of Northwest Portland. At one point, you can actually take in five stairways sequentially from N.W. Marshall to N.W. Quimby. N.W. Irving and N.W. Lovejoy also have stairways; they just don't fit as neatly into the Alphabet Walk.

Between 1865 and 1891, Northwest Portland was simply known as the Alphabet District. The streets were laid out on "True North" by Captain John Heard Couch. All the east-west streets were named successive letters in the alphabet and all the north-south streets were sequentially numbered, e.g. First Street, Second Street, Third Street and so on. It wasn't until the "Great Renaming of 1891" that names of prominent Portland people were thrown in a hat and the northwest street names — the ones we love to memorize if only to impress ourselves — were chosen.

Northwest Portland *Alphabet District*

N.W. Irving Street up to N.W. Westover Road
Year Built: Unknown
Number of Stairs: 48
Top Locator: 2470 N.W. Westover Rd.
Bottom Locator: N.W. Irving St. dead-end
Thomas Guide: 596, 5-C

Directions: From Pioneer Square (S.W. Broadway and S.W. Morrison St.), take S.W. Morrison St. west to S.W. 10th Ave. and make a right. Then make a left on W. Burnside St. Go up to N.W. 23rd Ave. and turn right. At N.W. Irving St. make a left. The street will dead-end past N.W. 24th Ave.

❦ This concrete stairway with a pipe railing will take you up to N.W. Westover Rd. If you want to continue to the Westover-Barker stairs, turn right at the top of the stairs and follow N.W. Westover Rd. past the N.W. Johnson, N.W. 25th Ave. and N.W. Westover intersection. This is a particularly busy three-way intersection during rush hour. Proceed with caution. The top of the stairs is directly ahead.

❦ During the "Great Renaming of 1891," there was a dearth of notable Portlanders with the last name beginning with the letter "I." Captain William Irving won the street by default even though he lived in Portland fewer than 10 years. Famous in Pacific Northwest maritime circles, Irving moved his Scottish family to Portland in 1849. He built a thriving steamboat business along the Willamette River and acquired a square-mile claim on the east side of town. Irving moved to British Columbia in 1858 and is credited with building the first steamboat in the province. He died in 1887 at the age of 56 and his heirs were among those who developed the "Irvington" subdivision in 1887.

Northwest Portland *Alphabet District*

N.W. Westover Road down to N.W. Barker Avenue (25th Place)
Year Built: 1983
Number of Stairs: 41
Top Locator: 2539 N.W. Westover Rd.
Bottom Locator: N.W. Barker Ave. dead-end
Thomas Guide: 596, 5-C

Directions: From Pioneer Square (S.W. Broadway and S.W. Morrison St.), take S.W. Morrison St. west to S.W. 10th Ave. and make a right. Then turn left on W. Burnside St. Go up to N.W. 23rd Ave. and turn right. At N.W. Flanders St. make a left. Turn right at N.W. Westover Road. The top of the stairs is on the right side of the street just before N.W. Westover turns up the hill.

❦ This is quick romp of concrete stairs has three landings, with the bottommost landing splitting the stairs off to the left and right. N.W. Barker Ave. is no more than a block long and if you want to continue your walk to the next stairway, go out to N.W. Lovejoy and turn left or west up the hill. Continue up N.W. Lovejoy to the end of the street. That's where the stairs begin.

A vintage 1911 tudor house sits next to the Westover-Barker stairs

Northwest Portland *Alphabet District*

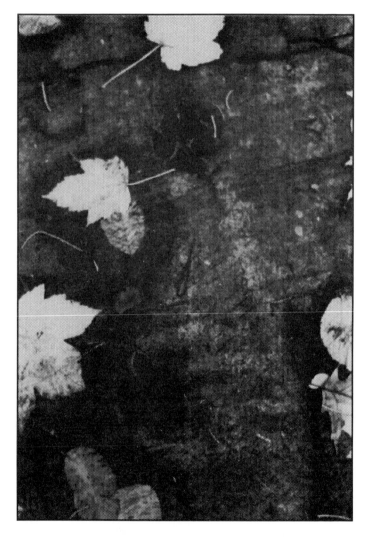

Take pause at the huge paws imbedded in the street at the base of the Lovejoy Stairs.

Northwest Portland *Alphabet District*

N.W. Lovejoy Street up to N.W. Summit Avenue
Year Built: Unknown
Number of Stairs: 34
Top Locator: 860 N.W. Summit Ave.
Bottom Locator: N.W. Lovejoy St. dead-end
Thomas Guide: 596, C-4

Directions: From Pioneer Square (S.W. Broadway and S.W. Morrison St.), take S.W. Morrison St. west to S.W. 10th Ave. and make a right. Then turn left on W. Burnside. Go up to N.W. 23rd Ave. and turn right. At N.W. Lovejoy St., make a left. Follow the street all the way to the end. The stairs begin just at the end of the street.

❦ This quiet little stairway is the first stretch of a combined route of three stairways, several sidewalks and two Forest Park Trails that will eventually take you all the way up to Pittock Mansion. This trek is a serious vertical challenge that takes about a 90-minute round trip.

❦ If the votes had gone another way during the "Great Renaming of 1891," we'd be referring to N.W. Lovejoy St. as N.W. Lewis St., after Meriwether Lewis. Lawrence Lovejoy made the alphabet team because of his civic contributions to the city of Portland from 1873 until he died at the age of 74 in 1882. Lovejoy was the director of Oregon's first telegraph company, one of the founders of the Oregon City Woolen Mills and a key organizer of the state's first Masonic Lodge.

Northwest Portland *Alphabet District*

Marshall-Cornell Stairs

Northwest Portland *Alphabet District*

N.W. Marshall Street up to N.W. Cornell Road
Year Built: 1988
Number of Stairs: 50
Top Locator: 2621 Cornell Rd.
Bottom Locator: N.W. Marshall St. dead-end
Thomas Guide: 596, C-4

Directions: From Pioneer Square (S.W. Broadway and S.W. Morrison St.), take S.W. Morrison St. west to S.W. 10th Ave. and make a right. Then make a left on W. Burnside St. Go up to N.W. 23rd Ave. and turn right. At N.W. Marshall St. make a left. The base of the stairs is located at the end of N.W. Marshall St., just past N.W. 26th Ave.

❦ If you choose to walk from the Lovejoy stairs, return down the stairs and walk back to the corner of N.W. Lovejoy St. and N.W. Cornell Road. Take N.W. Cornell Rd. up the hill or north for about a block. You'll see the top of the Marshall stairs on the right side of the street, next to the #18 bus stop.

❦ The Marshall stairs mark the beginning of the "Alphabet Walk" in which you can link five stairways—Marshall to Quimby—together from N.W. Cornell Rd. The Marshall stairs feature a circle planter on one of the landings. The planter has been known to lie fallow or choked with weeds. At other times, there's cheery abundance of wild flowers.

❦ Will the real Marshall please stand up? Over the years, there's been some confusion about which Marshall of Portland was honored with a street name. Erroneous accounts in newspaper articles claim that the northwest street was named for George Marshall. Others said Tom Marshall. But the general consensus is that Captain John Marshall is the real fellow for whom the street is named. Marshall came to Oregon from England when he was a mere 15 years old. A 1921 *Oregonian* interview with Marshall indicated that he enjoyed a long career as a riverboat captain on the Willamette. He was still vital at 84 and happily living on his namesake street.

Northwest Portland *Alphabet District*

Hemingway slept here; not on the stairs but in the house.

Northwest Portland *Alphabet District*

N.W. Northrup Street up to N.W. Cornell Road
Year Built: 1988
Number of Stairs: 51
Top Locator: 2651 Cornell Rd.
Bottom Locator: N.W. Northrup St. dead-end
Thomas Guide: 596, C-4

Directions: From Pioneer Square (S.W. Broadway and S.W. Morrison St.), take S.W. Morrison St. west to S.W. 10th Ave. and make a right. Then make a left on W. Burnside St. Go up to N.W. 23rd Ave. and turn right. At N.W. Northrup St., turn left and go all the way to the end of the street, past the N.W. 26th Ave. intersection. The stairs are at the end of the street.

❦ If you're coming from the Marshall stairs, walk back up the stairs to N.W. Cornell Rd. and go up another block due north. The stairs are on the east side of the street, just beyond the Gedney Gardens Bed and Breakfast sign.

❦ This little stairway includes a couple of landings and then you'll hit a wide walkway that passes by the Gedney Gardens Bed & Breakfast. The Gedney grounds are pretty, featuring a rich collection of dahlia blooms for summer color. Daphne odora brightens up the winter.

❦ Pioneer businessman Edward J. Northrup was honored with a namesake street during the "Great Renaming of 1891." Northrup came to Portland from the state of New York in 1852. He was an enterprising man who succeeded in several business ventures, including running hardware stores and building carriages and wagons. He was well respected in the community and was elected the president of the Portland Young Men's Christian Association.

Gedney Garden Stairs

Northwest Portland *Alphabet District*

*The Garden God closely watches the passerbys
on the Overton-Cornell Stairs.*

Northwest Portland *Alphabet District*

N.W. Overton Street up to Cornell Road
Year Built: 1927
Number of Stairs: 56
Top Locator: 2687 Cornell Rd.
Bottom Locator: N.W. Overton St. dead-end
Thomas Guide: 596, C-4

Directions: From Pioneer Square (S.W. Broadway and S.W. Morrison St.), take S.W. Morrison St. west to S.W. 10th Ave. and make a right. Then turn left on W. Burnside St. Go up to N.W. 23rd Ave. and turn right. At N.W. Overton St., turn left and continue past the N.W. 27th Ave. intersection. The stairs are at the end of N.W. Overton St.

❦ If you're coming from the Northrup stairs, walk back up the stairs to N.W. Cornell Rd. and go up another block due north. The stairs are on the east side of the street, past the 2687 N.W. Cornell Rd. address.

❦ From N.W. Cornell Rd., the stairs head down and empty onto a walkway that curves around a shady garden guarded by rusty iron gate "Garden God." An otherwise utilitarian fence surrounding the garden is topped with miniature lanterns. The garden jumps over to the other side of the walkway and down the remaining stairs. Blackberry brambles mix it up with the vegetable garden.

❦ As the first person to see and lay claim to what is now Portland, William Overton was the natural choice for a street name during the "Great Renaming of 1891." But Overton didn't let any Oregon moss grow under his feet. He only stayed on his claim a year and then left for California.

Northwest Portland *Alphabet District*

Pettygrove-Cornell Stairs

N.W. Pettygrove Street up to N.W. Cornell Road
Year Built: 1950
Number of Stairs: 61
Top Locator: 2747 Cornell Rd.
Bottom Locator: N.W. Pettygrove St. dead-end
Thomas Guide: 596, C-4

Directions: From Pioneer Square (S.W. Broadway and S.W. Morrison St.), take S.W. Morrison St. west to S.W. 10th Ave. and make a right. Then turn left on W. Burnside St. Go up to N.W. 23rd and turn right. At N.W. Pettygrove St., turn left and continue past the N.W. 27th Ave. intersection. The stairs are at the end of N.W. Pettygrove St.

❦ This stairway is just a hop from the Overton stairs. Continue north on N.W. Cornell Rd. and look for the school crossing on the east side of the street. The stairway is to your right.

❦ The Pettygrove stairs are part of a commuting path Chapman Elementary School kids heading to and from school. This is a very narrow stairway, featuring three short landings and a single railing for clinging, if necessary.

❦ Francis W. Pettygrove had quite a bit of competition in the "Great Renaming of 1891." Penn, Post , Powell and Pratt were candidates too. But these "P's" can't take credit for naming our fair city. Lovejoy of Massachusetts wanted to name the town Boston. Maine-native Pettygrove thought Portland was a better choice. A coin toss settled the debate. But Pettygrove didn't stay long in Portland to savor his win. After only four years in the Northwest, he left for California in 1849 in search of gold. Pettygrove did return to the Northwest a couple of years later and lived out his days in Port Townsend, Washington.

Northwest Portland *Alphabet District*

One of the many magnificent homes around the Quimby-Cornell stairs.

Northwest Portland *Alphabet District*

N.W. Quimby Street up to N.W. Cornell Road
Year Built: 1967
Number of Stairs: 25
Top Locator: 2865 Cornell Rd.
Bottom Locator: N.W. Quimby St. dead-end
Thomas Guide: 596, C-4

Directions: From Pioneer Square (S.W. Broadway and S.W. Morrison St.), take S.W. Morrison St. west to S.W. 10th Ave. and make a right. Then turn left on W. Burnside St. Go up to N.W. 23rd Ave. and turn right. At N.W. Lovejoy St., turn left and go up the hill, following the street to the right instead of continuing straight ahead to the Lovejoy steps. You are now on N.W. Cornell Rd. Go along N.W. Cornell Rd. past all the stairways, and turn right on easy-to-miss N.W. 30th Ave. Follow N.W. 30th Ave. around and you'll find the stairs at the end of the street.

🍎 N.W. Quimby St. is chopped up into several sections in the Alphabet District and this is the last appearance the street makes due west. The Quimby-Cornell stairs are a great find if only for the discovery of this quiet, tucked-away neighborhood. There are some splendid homes from the early 1900's and beautiful gardens to view.

🍎 L. P. W. Quimby was involved in Portland's booming "hospitality" business in the 1870's. According to the 1873 City Directory, there were 75 saloons and the population was only 15,000 — interesting ratio. Over the years, Quimby's business steadily grew and when it came time for the "Great Renaming of 1891," Quimby seemed a natural. He also had little competition in the "Q" department.

*Quimby-Cornell
Stairs*

Northwest Portland *Alphabet District*

Cornell-Summit Stairs

Northwest Portland *Alphabet District*

N.W. Cornell Road up to N.W. Summit Avenue
Year Built: Around 1914
Number of Stairs: 68
Top Locator: N.W. Summit Ave.
Bottom Locator: 2820 N.W. Cornell Rd.
Thomas Guide: 596, C-4

Directions: From Pioneer Square (S.W. Broadway and S.W. Morrison St.), take S.W. Morrison St. west to S.W. 10th Ave. and make a right. Then turn left on W. Burnside St. Go up to N.W. 23rd Ave. and turn right. At N.W. Lovejoy St., turn left and go up the hill and follow the street to the right. The street turns into N.W. Cornell Rd. Go along N.W. Cornell Rd. for about a 1/4 mile and the base of the stairs is on the left or west side of the street, just before the N.W. Cornell Rd. turns west up the hill.

❦ This Cornell-Summit stairway is the only one along N.W. Cornell Rd. that begins on the west side of the street. The stairway is listed in the Oregon Resource Directory in the area of landscape architecture. Worn risers and mossy walls doesn't seem to deter the Kings Heights kids from bounding down the stairs on their way to Chapman School down in the northwest flatlands.

Northwest Portland *Kings Heights*

Summit-Westover Stairs

N.W. Summit Avenue up to N.W. Westover Road
Year Built: Around 1914
Number of Stairs: 153
Top Locator: 2763 N.W. Westover Rd.
Bottom Locator: Corner of N.W. Summit Ave. and N.W. Cornell Rd.
Thomas Guide: 596, C-4

Directions: From Pioneer Square (S.W. Broadway and S.W. Morrison St.), take S.W. Morrison St. west to S.W. 10th Ave. and make a right. Then turn left on W. Burnside St. Go up to N.W. 23rd and turn right. At N.W. Lovejoy, turn left and go up the hill, following the street to the right. Now you're on N.W. Cornell Rd. The first street you're allowed to take a left on is S.W. Summit Ave. The turn is about an 1/8 of a mile from N.W. Lovejoy St. Make a hairpin left onto N.W. Summit. The stairs show up immediately on the right or west side of the street.

❦ It's much easier to get to this stairway from the Lovejoy stairs. Make a right at the top of the stairs on N.W. Summit Ave. and you'll see the stairs to your left before the street meets up with N.W. Cornell Rd.

❦ These stairs are a relentless rise up to N.W. Westover Rd. Should you become winded during the ascent, there are set-in benches or "cardiac rests" on each landing.

❦ Runaway gardens offer dense, shady cover and vine maple bursts with great fall color. English ivy runs wild alongside other woodland plants such as sword fern and Solomon's seal At the top, look out to the north where Mt. Saint Helens majestically greets you on a clear day.

Summit-Westover Stairs

Northwest Portland *Kings Heights*

Fairfax-Cumberland Stairs

Northwest Portland *Kings Heights*

N.W. Fairfax Terrace up to N.W. Cumberland Road
Year Built: 1914
Number of Stairs: 127
Top Locator: 2839 N.W. Cumberland Rd.
Bottom Locator: Corner of N.W. Fairfax Ter. and N.W. Cumberland Rd.
Thomas Guide: 596, C-4

Directions: From Pioneer Square (S.W. Broadway and S.W. Morrison St.), take S.W. Morrison St. west to S.W. 10th Ave. and make a right. Then turn left on W. Burnside St. Go up to N.W. 23rd Ave. and turn right. At N.W. Lovejoy St., turn left and go up the hill, following the street to the right. You're now on N.W. Cornell Road. At the first stop sign, turn left or south on N.W. Westover Rd. It gets a little tricky here but just keep staying to your right as you go up the hill. Look for the intersection of N.W. Westover Rd., N.W. Cumberland Rd. and N.W. Fairfax Ter. The bottom of the stairs are located on the west side of N.W. Fairfax Ter.

❦ This stairway is another pulmonary pounder. There are plenty of risers but the walkway between stair flights is a welcome reprieve. The stairs are shaded by shrubs and by a large, established Japanese maple that looks exquisite in the snow. Along the walkway you'll see lush sedum, hosta and houttuynia. Cotoneaster, St. John's wort and rhododendrons come into play further up the stairs.

Northwest Portland *Kings Heights*

Bounding down ivy-bound Luray stairs.

Northwest Portland *Kings Heights*

N.W. Luray Terrace up to N.W. Luray Circus
Year Built: Unknown
Number of Stairs: 53
Top Locator: 3002 Luray Cir.
Bottom Locator: 2915 N.W. Luray Ter.
Thomas Guide: 596, C-4

Directions: From Pioneer Square (S.W. Broadway and S.W. Morrison St.), take S.W. Morrison St. west to S.W. 10th Ave. and make a right. Then turn left on W. Burnside. Go up to N.W. 23rd Ave. and turn right. At N.W. Lovejoy St., turn left, go up the hill, following the street to the right. You're now on N.W. Cornell Rd. At the first stop sign, turn left or south onto N.W. Westover Rd. Continue to the right and you'll be on N.W. Cumberland Rd. Make a right on N.W. Luray (rhymes with Hooray) Ter. The stairs are on the left or west side of the street.

❦ This is another great, out-of-the-way stairway in Kings Heights. But rarely can you approach these stairs undetected by an enthusiastic standard poodle that lives next door. Bouncing and barking is definitely part of his job description.

❦ The shady nature of this stairway makes for a perfect summer walk. You'll note a contrast between the overgrown, let-nature-take-its-course foliage on the stairs and the beautifully manicured garden of rhododendrons and shade-loving plants up on Luray Circus.

Northwest Portland *Kings Heights*

"Ariel Terraces" on N.W. Cumberland was formerly the home of Clarissa Inman, inventor of the electric curling iron. It's rumored that the mansion is haunted. Documented manifestations are eerie enough to make your hair curl.

Ariel Terraces on
N.W. Cumberland Road.

Northwest Portland *Kings Heights*

Hit The Heights

❦ If you're in the mood for a serious stair-stepping adventure, you'll want to take this walk from the Lovejoy Stairs up to Pittock Mansion. The trek covers three stairways, several sidewalks and two Forest Park Trails. The round trip takes about 90 minutes.

❦ From the top of the Lovejoy stairs, turn right on N.W. Summit Ave. and head down the block. The next set of stairs begins on N.W. Summit Ave., right before the street meets up with N.W. Cornell Rd. The opening to the stairs will be on the left side of the street. The road at the top of the stairs is N.W. Westover Rd. Continue west across the street and you'll see the N.W. Fairfax Ter. stairs. These stairs will take you up to N.W. Cumberland Rd. Follow N.W. Cumberland Rd. up the hill all the way to where it dead-ends. The Cumberland Trail begins here. Take this path to Wildwood Trail and follow Wildwood Trail up to Pittock Mansion.

Northwest Portland *King's Heights*

Pittock Gate House Stairs

Northwest Portland *King's Heights*

Pittock Mansion down to the Gatehouse
Year Built: Around 1914
Number of Stairs: 24
Top Locator: Pittock Mansion, south side
Bottom Locator: Pittock Gatehouse
Thomas Guide: 596, 5-B

Directions: From Pioneer Square (S.W. Broadway and S.W. Morrison St.), take S.W. Morrison St. west to S.W. 10th Ave. Turn right. Go to W. Burnside St. and turn left. Take W. Burnside St. up past Uptown Shopping Center (N.W. 23rd Ave. and W. Burnside St.) and follow the signs to Pittock Mansion. It's about two miles from downtown. Parking is ample. The stairs are on the south side of the house.

❧ One of the city's more popular tourist attractions, Pittock Mansion, harkens back to the elegant civility of a bygone era. The "chateauesque" architectural style, manicured gardens and rolling lawn are exquisite. While there is a price of admission for the indoor tour, there's no charge for peeking in through the mansion's windows at the well-preserved opulence. The stairs are hidden off to the south side of the house and take you down to the Gate Lodge where lunch and tea are genteelly served.

❧ Completed in 1914, Pittock Mansion was the dream home of *Oregonian* publisher Henry Pittock. At that time, the locale was the highest residential site accessible by car and commanded a breathtaking 180-degree view. One story has it that Pittock compromised mightily to acquire his lofty lot. A young politician, Phil Metschan, Jr. owned the property and was planning to build a grandiose hotel call the Imperial House on the site. The name mirrored the Metschan family's successful downtown Imperial Hotel. Pittock eventually persuaded Metschan to sell by promising *Oregonian* support of any political ventures that Metschan would henceforth pursue. While there is no hard proof of this agreement, Metschan did enjoy a long and successful political career and throughout, he received solid backing from the *Oregonian*.

Northwest Portland *Montgomery Park*

These stairs are a tribute to Bill Naito's perseverance.

Northwest Portland *Montgomery Park*

N.E. Wardway Street up to Montgomery Park
Year Built: 1996
Number of Stairs: 57
Top Locator: Montgomery Park parking lot
Bottom Locator: N.E. Wardway St. and N.W. Nicolai St. intersection
Thomas Guide: 596, C-3

Directions: From Pioneer Square (S.W. Broadway and S.W. Morrison St.), take S.W. Morrison St. west to S.W. 10th Ave. and make a right. Then make a left on W. Burnside St. Go up to N.W. 23rd Ave. and turn right. Drive past all the Alphabet streets to N.W. Vaughn St. and turn left. This street will turn into N.E. Wardway St. once you pass the main driveway to Montgomery Park on your right. The stairs are on the right side of the street, going up the ivy-covered hill. Look for the bright blue handrail.

❦ According to Montgomery Park building superintendent, Tom Kay, this stairway was a pet project of Bill Naito. Naito wanted a stairway that would provide access up to Montgomery Park from the lower parking lot on N.W. Nicolai St. Budget issues halted stair construction several times but Naito persevered and the project was eventually completed.

Northwest Portland *Montgomery Park*

This stairway gets an "A" for parallel structure.

Northwest Portland *Montgomery Park*

N.E. Wardway Street up to N.W. 28th Place
Year Built: 1988
Number of Stairs: 28
Top Locator: N.W. 28th Place dead-end
Bottom Locator: Montgomery Park
Thomas Guide: 596, C-3

Directions: From Pioneer Square (S.W. Broadway and S.W. Morrison St.), take S.W. Morrison west to S.W. 10th Ave. and make a right. Then make a left on W. Burnside St. Go up to N.W. 23rd Ave. and turn right. Drive past all the Alphabet streets to N.W. Vaughn St. and turn left. This street will turn into N.E. Wardway St. once you pass the main driveway to Montgomery Park on your right. The stairs are on the left side of the street, across from the Montgomery Park parking lot.

❦ These stairs are a help for the residents up on N.W. 28th Pl. They can also be easily combined with the Montgomery Park stairs across the street.

Northwest Portland *Willamette Heights*

Leaf-littered Stairs

Northwest Portland *Willamette Heights*

Willamette Heights

An early 1900's insurance map reads, "The situation of Willamette Heights is most sightly." Indeed, the steep hills north of Balch Creek commanded panoramic views and the developers were intent on creating a neighborhood where the newly affluent could live at the same elevation as the Portland Heights blue bloods. Beautiful homes were built and Willamette Heights was became an enviable address for many decades. Parts of Northwest Portland fell into disrepair during the 1960's and 1970's and, as a result, Willamette Heights slipped in neighborhood status. A focused renewal effort in the last 15 years, however, has successfully restored the area back to its original "sightly" status.

The Willamette Heights plat was filed by John Hale and his wife, California E. Hale in 1890. A wooden bridge was built to cross Balch Creek and N.W. Thurman St. soon became a major thoroughfare and trolley route. Not to be overlooked during the city-wide preparations for the Lewis & Clark Exposition, Willamette Heights residents petitioned to have a new bridge built. The Balch Creek Canyon Bridge, a steel, two-tower deck truss bridge, was built in 1905. Now called the Thurman Street Bridge, this structure is the oldest highway deck truss in Oregon. It is also one of two remaining pin-connected deck trusses in the state. The only major alternation to the bridge was made in the mid-1950's when a car slid on the icy bridge and crashed through the wrought-iron railing. A female passenger was killed. To prevent any more accidents, the railing was replaced by a steel guard rail and a cyclone fence was put in.

For the curious, "T" Street was renamed N.W. Thurman Street in honor of G. William Thurman, a pioneer family descendant and assistant manager of the Pacific Postal Telegraph Cable Co. If these credentials seem a little light, we come to find out that Thurman's buddy, Douglas Taylor, was the man in charge of the 1891 street renaming.

Northwest Portland *Willamette Heights*

MacLeay Park Stairs

Northwest Portland *Willamette Heights*

N.W. Thurman Street Bridge down to MacLeay Park
Year Built: 1986
Number of Stairs: 63
Top Locator: Thurman Bridge
Bottom Locator: MacLeay Park
Thomas Guide: 596, B-3

Directions: From Pioneer Square (S.W. Broadway and S.W. Morrison St.), take S.W. Morrison St. west to S.W. 10th Ave. and make a right. Then make a left on W. Burnside St. Go up to N.W. 23rd Ave. and turn right. Drive past all the Alphabet streets to N.W. Thurman St. Turn left on N.W. Thurman St. and head up the hill. The stairs begin on the northeast side of the Thurman Street Bridge.

❦ This stairway is a great way to quickly drop down to MacLeay Park. The stairs start out conventionally enough with concrete risers, then give way to railroad ties and terraced dirt stairs reinforced by wood slats. If you're in the mood for a real trek, you can catch the lower MacLeay Trail which will take you up to Wildwood Trail. Four miles later, you're at Pittock Mansion.

❦ Donated to the city in 1897, 130-acre MacLeay Park is a popular site for picnicking, hiking, etc. The Park has changed little over the years and still includes the original path system and the remains of an early Portland water works. Further up Lower MacLeay Trail, you'll find a stone restroom built in 1933 by the WPA.

Northwest Portland *Willamette Heights*

MacLeay Park 1912

The Ballad of Balch Creek

The creek running through MacLeay Park is Balch Creek, named after Danforth Balch, the first person to be legally hanged in Oregon. A native of Massachusetts, Balch arrived in Oregon in 1850 and staked out a 640-acre claim in the heavily wooded northwest part of Portland. Danforth and his wife, Mary Jane, had nine children. All was well with the Balch family until the day 16 year-old Anna Balch eloped to Vancouver, Washington with the Stump boy, Mortimer. When the newlyweds returned some days later, Balch and his shotgun were there to greet the Stumps at the Stark Street ferry. Words were exchanged and Balch shot Stump dead. As Balch was leaving the scene of the crime, Stump's father whacked Balch on the head with a pike pole. Balch was captured and hauled off to Portland's one-cell jail. Portland's 2,000 residents were appalled to hear of the incident. After all, this was 1859 and Portland was a civilized town where differences were no longer settled by shotguns. Balch was tried for murder. He was convicted, sentenced to death and was hanged on October 17, 1859.

After Danforth's death, Mary Jane Balch took up with John Confer, "a man of no account," according to *The Oregonian*. The alliance caused some legal problems with regard to land inheritance. The children ended up with nothing and Mary Jane ended up with the man of no account.

Northwest Portland *Willamette Heights*

N.W. Thurman Street down to N.W. Vaughn Street
Year Built: Unknown
Number of Stairs: 50
Top Locator: 3245 Thurman St.
Bottom Locator: 3304 N.W. Vaughn St.
Thomas Guide: 596, B-3

Directions: From Pioneer Square (S.W. Broadway and S.W. Morrison St.), take S.W. Morrison St. west to S.W. 10th Ave. and make a right. Then make a left on W. Burnside St. Go up to N.W. 23rd Ave. and turn right. Drive past all the Alphabet streets to N.W. Thurman St. Turn left on N.W. Thurman St. Head up the hill and over the Thurman Street Bridge. Once you're over the Thurman Street Bridge, start looking for the 3245 address.

❦ The asphalt driveway, just west of the 3245 N.W. Thurman brick house, leads to the first set of wood stairs. These stairs end up at a house with a fence. At this point, the walkway and stairs maneuver their way through some private backyards. Though walking this route may seem like trespassing, the city assures me that, according to each property deed along the route, the owners must allow public access. Even that asphalt driveway is on city property. Be bold and go forth!

Northwest Portland *Willamette Heights*

N.W. Thurman up to N.W. Aspen
Year Built: 1988
Number of Stairs: 101
Top Locator: 1836 N.W. Aspen
Bottom Locator: 3418 N.W. Thurman
Thomas Guide: 596, B-3

Directions: From Pioneer Square (S.W. Broadway and S.W. Morrison), take S.W. Morrison west to S.W. 10th Ave. and make a right. Then make a left on W. Burnside. Go up to N.W. 23rd and turn right. Go down through all the Alphabet streets to N.W. Thurman. Turn left on N.W. Thurman. Head up the hill and over the Thurman Street Bridge. The stairs are on the south side of the street. Watch for the 3418 address.

❧ These stairs make quick work of this hill, incorporating several landings and a nice walkway as you make your way up to N.W. Aspen. Tall, reedy bamboo bushes grace the pathway and further along you're shaded by a very large chestnut tree. If you want to catch a Forest Park Trail, make a left at the top of the stairs and walk down Aspen for just a bit. Aspen Trail starts on the west side of the street.

*Birdhouse
perched above
the stairs*

*Bamboo
abounds*

Northwest Portland *Linnton*

These ivy-covered stairs take you up to a long-forgotten place.

Northwest Portland *Linnton*

Linnton

Portland city limits due north extend well past the St. Johns bridge to just beyond the hillside community of Linnton. Platted out around 1843 by pioneers Peter H. Burnett and M.M. McCarver, Linnton was originally its own little town. It was named after Senator Lewis F. Linn of Missouri, a longtime cheerleader of American occupation of Oregon. Burnett had high hopes for the hillside community, declaring, "I have no doubt that this place will be the great commercial town of the territory." So much for his soothsaying skills. Some time afterward, Burnett pulled up stakes and headed into California where he rose to political prominence, becoming California's first governor.

While Linnton was merged into Portland in 1915, the town is still treated as a separate enclave from Portland proper. The community's isolation from the city is partly due to the heavy industry that runs along the river side all the way to Linnton. There's also 5,000-acre Forest Park on the west side of Saint Helens Road (Hwy 30) that separates Linnton from Northwest Portland.

Saint Helens Road is one big deafening whir of industrial traffic. Once you pass under the St. Johns Bridge, however, city planners have made a concession to the biped by building elevated sidewalks along the road. This walkway somewhat removes you from the fumes and gusts of grit but there is no escape from the din. It's only when you hit the stairs that you're transported up to quieter pockets of hillside civilization. Many of the stairways in the Linnton area have seen better days. There have been maintenance crews up there, however, and stair repair is a high priority.

Northwest Portland *Linnton*

The Saint Helens-Germantown Stairs

Northwest Portland *Linnton*

N.W. Saint Helens Road up to N.W. Germantown Road
Year Built: Unknown
Number of Stairs: 134
Top Locator: 9259 N.W. Germantown Rd.
Bottom Locator: N.W. Saint Helens Rd.
Thomas Guide: 565, E-3

Directions: From Pioneer Square (S.W. Broadway and S.W. Morrison St.),
take S.W. Morrison St. west up to S.W. 10th Ave. Turn right on S.W. 10th,
then make a left onto W. Burnside St. Turn right just past S.W. 14th Ave. and
get on I-405 due north. As you pass through the Pearl District and Northwest Portland, follow signs to Hwy 30. Take Hwy 30 — N.W. Saint Helens Rd.
— north past the St. Johns Bridge. There is an elevated sidewalk that begins
on the west side of the street. The base of the stairs starts midway down the
walk.

❧ This section of the stairs has fallen into great disrepair and you might
hazard a splinter or two from the chipped and peeling wood hand railing.
Attractions along the route include an abandoned house, trash, more trash
and blackberry bushes. The good news is that stair repair people have been
seen working on this stairway. New or at least sturdier risers will be an
improvement.

Northwest Portland *Linnton*

N.W. Saint Helens Road up to N.W. Roseway Avenue
Year Built: Unknown
Number of Stairs: 80
Top Locator: 9452 N.W. Roseway Ave.
Bottom Locator: Saint Helens Rd.
Thomas Guide: 565, E-3

Directions: From Pioneer Square (S.W. Broadway and S.W. Morrison St.), take S.W. Morrison St. west up to S.W. 10th Ave. Turn right on S.W. 10th, then make a left onto W. Burnside St. Turn right just past S.W. 14th Ave. and get on I-405 due north. As you pass through the Pearl District and Northwest Portland, follow signs to Hwy 30. Take Hwy. 30 — Saint Helens Rd. — north past the St. Johns Bridge. You'll first see the elevated sidewalk and the stairway up to N.W. Germantown on your left. The next set of stairs will take you up to N.W. Roseway Ave.

❦ If you need to park, turn left on Harbor Blvd. and follow the street around and up the hill. N.W. Harbor turns into N.W. Roseway Ave. Look for the 9452 address on the right side of the street and head down the stairs to N.W. Saint Helens Road.

❦ As you make your way up the hill from landing to landing, you'll see a water runoff area made of boulders. That must have been some raging rush of water during the 1996 flooding. Blackberry bushes have run riot throughout the area.

Northwest Portland *Linnton*

St. Helens Road up to N.W. Roseway Dead-end
Year Built: 1980
Number of Stairs: 65
Top Locator: 9663 N.W. Roseway
Bottom Locator: St. Helens Road
Thomas Guide: 565, E-3

Directions: From Pioneer Square (S.W. Broadway and S.W. Morrison St.), take S.W. Morrison St. west up to S.W. 10th Ave. Turn right on S.W. 10th, then make a left onto W. Burnside St. Turn right just past S.W. 14th Ave. and get on I-405 due north. As you pass through the Pearl District and Northwest Portland, follow signs to Hwy 30. Take Hwy. 30 — Saint Helens Rd. — north past the St. Johns Bridge. You'll first see the elevated walkway and then the stairway up to N.W. Germantown on your left. Next comes the first N.W. Roseway Ave. stairway. This stairway is your final stop.

❦ Again, for the motoring folks, take a left on N.W. Harbor Blvd. and follow the street up the hill and it will turn into N.W. Roseway Ave. Go down to the end of the street and you'll find the stairway on the right side of the street just past the blue cottage.

❦ Similar to the preceding stairway, these stairs also features several landings as it channels you between N.W. Roseway Ave. and N.W. Saint Helens Road. Great views.

Northwest Portland *Linnton*

N.W. Saint Helens Road up to N.W. Wilark Avenue
Year Built: 1982
Number of Stairs: 58
Top Locator: 10160 N.W. Wilark Ave.
Bottom Locator: N.W. Saint Helens Rd.
Thomas Guide: 565, E-2

Directions: From Pioneer Square (S.W. Broadway and S.W. Morrison St.), take S.W. Morrison St. west up to S.W. 10th Ave. Turn right on S.W. 10th, then make a left onto W. Burnside St. Turn right just past S.W. 14th Ave. and get on I-405 due north. As you pass through the Pearl District and Northwest Portland, follow signs to Hwy 30. Take Hwy. 30 — Saint Helens Rd. — north past the St. Johns Bridge and the first series of stairways on the elevated sidewalk. At the corner of N.W. Hoge Ave. and N.W. Saint Helens Rd., you'll see 44 steps going up the hill. They stop abruptly, leading to nowhere. Continue along the sidewalk and you'll see the beginning of the Wilark stairs.

❦ If you're driving, you can make a left on N.W. Hoge, then right on N.W. Wilark Ave. The stairs will be on the right side of the street and they'll take you down to N.W. Saint Helens Rd. Whether you go up or down the stairs, you'll pass by some holly and shady overhanging foliage. The top of the stairs offers vistas of Mt. Rainier, Mt. Saint Helens and Mt. Adams. A spectacular view, weather permitting.

Northwest Portland *Linnton*

N.W. Saint Helens Road up to N.W. 2nd Street
Year Built: Unknown
Number of Stairs: 106
Top Locator: N.W. 2nd St. dead-end
Bottom Locator: N.W. Saint Helens Rd.
Thomas Guide: 565, E-2

Directions: From Pioneer Square (S.W. Broadway and S.W. Morrison St.), take S.W. Morrison St. west up to S.W. 10th Ave. Turn right on S.W. 10th, then make a left onto W. Burnside St. Turn right just past S.W. 14th Ave. and get on I-405 due north. As you pass through the Pearl District and Northwest Portland, follow signs to Hwy 30. Take Hwy. 30 — Saint Helens Rd. — north past the St. Johns Bridge. After about two miles, you'll see a turnout on the left side of the street. You may park there. Follow the sidewalk due north and you'll see the beginning of the stairs, going up the hill

❦ Linnton School was indeed a learning institution at one time. After some years of being abandoned, an enterprising renovator transformed the block-of-brick building into exclusive condominiums, guarded by a impenetrable-looking gate. The stair walker is welcome to gaze at the well-maintained grounds from the other side of the gate or fence. Sometimes you can even catch a glimpse of Scottish Terriers running amuck.

The Linnton School Condominiums

Northwest Portland *Linnton*

N.W. Saint Helens Road up to N.W. 3rd Street
Year Built: 1982 (first set); 1964 (second set)
Number of Stairs: 180
Top locator: N.W. 107th Ave. and N.W. 3rd St.
Bottom Locator: N.W. 107th Ave. and N.W. Saint Helens Rd.
Thomas Guide: 565, E-2

Directions: From Pioneer Square (S.W. Broadway and S.W. Morrison St.), take S.W. Morrison St. west up to S.W. 10th Ave. Turn right on S.W. 10th, then make a left onto W. Burnside St. Turn right just past S.W. 14th Ave. and get on I-405 due north. As you pass through the Pearl District and Northwest Portland, follow signs to Hwy 30. Take Hwy. 30 — Saint Helens Rd. — north past the St. Johns Bridge. At about two miles north past St. Johns Bridge, you'll see the Linnton Community Center on your right. You may park on that side of the road and cross the street at the crosswalk. The stairs are right in front of you.

❦ This is a handy stairway for Linnton residents who elect to take the bus into town. The stairs take you up past N.W. 1st St., N.W. 2nd St. and eventually up to N.W. 3rd St. Runaway blackberry bushes cover one hillside next to the stairs and well-tended gardens appear on the right. In the middle of the stair climb, you'll see a beautiful, mature weeping willow tree.

N.W. 1st Street up to N.W. 3rd Street
Year Built: 1965
Number of Stairs: 92
Top Locator: N.W. 108th Ave. and N.W. 3rd St.
Bottom Locator: N.W. 108th Ave. and N.W. 1st St.
Thomas Guide: 565, D-2

Directions: From Pioneer Square (S.W. Broadway and S.W. Morrison St.), take S.W. Morrison St. west up to S.W. 10th Ave. Turn right on S.W. 10th, then make a left onto W. Burnside St. Turn right just past S.W. 14th Ave. and get on I-405 due north. As you pass through the Pearl District and Northwest Portland, follow signs to Hwy 30. Take Hwy. 30 — Saint Helens Rd. — north past the St. Johns Bridge. After two miles, you'll see the Linnton Community Center on your right and N.W. 112th Ave. on your left. Turn left on N.W. 112th Ave. and head up the hill. Make a hairpin right onto N.W. 108th Ave. You'll see a curved retaining wall on your right. The first set of eight stairs will take you up to a walkway that turns up the hill to six consecutive flights of stairs.

❧ Sometimes these funny, narrow streets can only accommodate one car at a time. If you're driving up in this area, be careful where you park so you don't block the street or a driveway.

Northwest Portland *Linnton*

Lots and lots of Linnton Stairs

Northwest Portland *Linnton*

N.W. 1st Street up to N.W. 3rd Street
Year Built: 1970
Number of Stairs: 56
Top Locator: N.W. 3rd St. and N.W. 109 Ave.
Bottom Locator: N.W. 1st St. and N.W. 109 Ave.
Thomas Guide: 565, D-1

Directions: From Pioneer Square (S.W. Broadway and S.W. Morrison St.), take S.W. Morrison St. west up to S.W. 10th Ave. Turn right on S.W. 10th, then make a left onto W. Burnside St. Turn right just past S.W. 14th Ave. and get on I-405 due north. As you pass through the Pearl District and Northwest Portland, follow signs to Hwy 30. Take Hwy. 30 — Saint Helens Rd. — north past the St. Johns Bridge. After two miles, you'll see the Linnton Community Center on your right and N.W. 112th Ave. on your left. Turn left on N.W. 112th Ave. and head up the hill. The stairway is to your right at the intersection of N.W. 1st St. and N.W. 109th. If you're coming from the base of the previous stairs, just continue along N.W. First and you'll see the stairs on your left.

❧ Cute hillside houses with pretty little perennial gardens grow alongside these stairs. Blackberry bushes monopolize some of the hillside but you can still find some bright poppies at the bottom of the stairs.

Southwest Portland *OHSU*

"Pill Hill"

Oregon Health Sciences University, commonly known as "Pill Hill," is situated on Marquam Hill off of Terwilliger Blvd. The building of a Medical School was conceived in 1913 by then Dean of the University Of Oregon Medical School, Dr. Kenneth A.J. Mackenzie. The concept was to create an "acropolis," replete with Parthenonesque structures of higher learning set against a lush Northwest backdrop. The University of Oregon Medical School moved from its modest location near Good Samaritan to the highlands in 1919. Donations of property throughout the development of the Medical School, the hospital and other facilities were extensive but none was so generous as the 88-acre gift from the *Oregon Journal* publisher, Charles Samuel Jackson, in 1924. Jackson died three days later after the land was donated to the state as a Christmas gift on December 24th. He was 64.

Sources say that not a year has gone by when there hasn't been some building project in the works. Marquam Hill continues to be in a perpetual state of construction either in the lower campus, home to the School of Dentistry and Casey Eye Institute or up in the higher elevations where the original buildings still stand. The latest construction venture is the new Doernbecher Children's Hospital. It will span across Campus Drive from the existing Children's Hospital and over to S.W. Veterans Hospital Road. Prior to the groundbreaking of the Doernbecher project, there was an excellent stair trail that originated at the base of the hill across the street from the School of Dentistry. It went straight up the hill, ending up across the street from the Campus Services Building on S.W. Veterans Hospital Road. The stairs were hidden by towering trees and heavy undergrowth and the risers were also erratically spaced, giving you the feeling of being in the middle of an orienteering course. The remaining vestige of trail is a winding bark dust path that runs from a S.W. Campus Drive parking structure up to the south side of the footbridge.

Southwest Portland *OHSU*

The stairs at OHSU will take you by both old and new architectural wonders. The massive, blue accordion-like VA building, for example, is nationally renowned for its skybridge. Opened in 1991, the Veteran's Hospital Skybridge is—at 660 feet—the longest air-conditioned pedestrian bridge in the United States. Older Parthenon-like structures built during the second decade of the 20th century can be found further up the hill off of Sam Jackson Park Road. All in all, the old and new seem to happily coexist up on the hill with little jarring to one's architectural sensibilities.

The key challenge for the stair-seeker is not how to get about this vertical acreage but where to park. Most every parking lot and structure is restricted to students, faculty or patients. In other words, the limited parking is for people who have business up here. Your best bet is to park along the perimeter of the campus. That means parking on S.W. Terwilliger around Campus Drive or further south on Terwilliger, around S.W. Condor. There's also two-hour visitor parking available along S.W. Gaines.

Many of the directions to stairs in this chapter include directions from other stairs in the area. Since you're up there, you may as well get the full vertical impact.

Southwest Portland *OHSU*

The Condor Stairs

Southwest Portland *OHSU*

S. W. Condor and S.W. Terwilliger up to the VA Hospital Bldg. 16
Year Built: Around 1928
Number of Stairs: 90
Top Locator: VA Building 16 Parking Lot
Bottom Locator: S.W. Condor Street and S.W. Terwilliger Blvd.
(northeast side of street, opposite stairs)
Thomas Guide: 626, E-2

Directions: From Pioneer Square (S.W. Broadway and S.W. Yamhill St.),
take S.W. Broadway due south out of downtown and past Portland State
University. As you go over I-405, S.W. 6th Ave. turns into S.W. Terwilliger.
To head up the hill, however, get in the left-hand turn lane and make a left
at the intersection of S.W. Sam Jackson Park Road and S.W. Terwilliger.
Continue along the road for about a mile. At this point, you'll pass S.W.
Condor Street on your left and you'll see the stairs on your right. There is a
parking turn-out on the left or east side of the street just past the stairs.
CAUTION: There's a blind curve along here and even though a crosswalk is
provided at the southeast corner of S.W. Condor and S.W. Terwilliger, it's
still a tricky crossing. Look both ways two or three times before crossing.

❦ These stairs are well-known among the Pill Hill gang and they're a
popular add-on workout for the Terwilliger runners and walkers. If you are
in the exercise mode, it's very likely you'll unknowingly whiz by the Spanish
War Veterans Memorial just off to the right (11th landing), before you reach
the top of the stairs. Dedicated on September 13, 1938, the memorial is set
back about 50 yards from the stairs. The center piece looks like a worn,
mini-altar. To either side of the memorial are two rose-colored marble
benches. Heavily shaded under a canopy of trees, the memorial is a noble
remembrance that quietly asks us to give pause.

Southwest Portland *OHSU*

Building 16 Parking Lot up to the VA Hospital
Year Built: Unknown
Number of Stairs: 72
Top Locator: VA Hospital
Bottom Locator: Building 16 Parking Lot (Top of S.W. Condor Stairs)
Thomas Guide: 626, E-2

Directions: Parking problems for the lay person persist here so it's best to approach the stairs from the S.W. Condor stairs off of S.W. Terwilliger. Once you're on the S.W. Condor stairs, continue to the top. When the stairs break out to the right and left of the large, round stone wall, take the stairs to the right. Make your way on a diagonal to the right across the parking lot. There's a set of wood stairs that leads to an asphalt path. The path will meet another set of 31 stairs up to the left. The last flight of 22 stairs will empty out onto the VA parking lot.

❦ Once you make it up the first set of stairs, the surroundings change to a pleasant wooded area complete with picnic benches.

Southwest Portland *OHSU*

S.W. Gaines down to the Campus Services Building
Year Built: Unknown
Number of Stairs: 70
Top Locator: West side of Campus Services Building
Bottom Locator: 3505 S.W. Veterans Hospital Road
Thomas Guide: 626, D-2

Directions: From Pioneer Square (S.W. Broadway and S.W. Yamhill), take S.W. Broadway due south out of downtown and past Portland State University. As you go over I-405, S.W. 6th turns into S.W. Terwilliger. To head up the hill, however, get in the left-hand turn lane and make a left at the intersection of S.W. Sam Jackson Park Road and S.W. Terwilliger. Continue along the road past S.W. Campus Drive and take the next available rigth at S.W. Veterans Hospital Road. Then make another right onto S.W. Gaines. Continue on S.W. Gaines until you reach the S.W. 9th Ave. street sign. The stairs begin between the new School of Nursing and the old School of Nursing, now the Campus Service Building.

❦ Follow the walkway to the left between the buildings, always keeping close to the Campus Services Building on your right. The first set of very narrow stairs takes you to a path behind the building. From there, follow the outline of the building and you'll finally end up at the loading dock and S.W. Veterans Hospital Road. The only available parking is further up in the more residential section of S.W. Gaines.

❦ The OHSU official types were wary about mentioning this succession of steps that takes you down behind the old School of Nursing, now the Campus Services Building. After all, the stairs are old, narrow and uneven. But that's why we like them. This same series of stairs that unceremoniously drops you down to the loading dock also completes the loop back to the new School of Nursing stairs. Now we like them all the more. In an effort to appease the powers that be, please use your noggin and don't do anything stupid like roller skate down these stairs. If some accident should befall you, traction isn't far away.

Southwest Portland *OHSU*

Buster the Lemming

Southwest Portland *OHSU*

S.W. Gaines down to the School Of Nursing
Year Built: Unknown
Number of Stairs: 106
Top Locator: S.W. Gaines and S.W. 9th
Bottom Locator: 3455 S.W. Veterans Hospital Road
Thomas Guide: 626, D-2

Directions: From Pioneer Square (S.W. Broadway and S.W. Yamhill), take
S.W. Broadway due south out of downtown and past Portland State
University. As you go over I-405, S.W. 6th turns into S.W. Terwilliger. To
head up the hill, however, get in the left-hand turn lane and make a left at
the intersection of S.W. Sam Jackson Park Road and S.W. Terwilliger.
Duniway Park will be on your left. Continue along the road past S.W.
Campus Drive. The next available right is S.W. Veterans Hospital Road. Turn
right. Make another right onto S.W. Gaines. You'll see the top of the stairs
just past the upper entrance to the new School of Nursing. The only
available parking is further up in the more residential section of S.W. Gaines.

Some OHSU stairs are roped off as a
precaution during inclement weather.

Southwest Portland *OHSU*

It's an easy glide down to the Sports & Fitness Center.

Southwest Portland *OHSU*

BICC Building to Fitness and Sports Center
Year Built: Unknown
Number of Stairs: 179
Top Locator: 3300 S.W. Sam Jackson Park Road (rear of BICC Building)
Bottom Locator: Front of Fitness and Sports Center (S.W. Campus Drive)
Thomas Guide: 626, E-2

Directions: From Pioneer Square (S.W. Broadway and S.W. Yamhill), take S.W. Broadway due south through downtown and past Portland State University. As you go over I-405, S.W. 6th turns into S.W. Terwilliger. At the second light, instead of turning left up the hill on S.W. Terwilliger Blvd., continue straight ahead and you'll be on S.W. Sam Jackson Park Road. Follow the road up the hill and the BICC Building (Biomedical Information Communications Center) will be at the crest of the hill on your left. The stairs begin on the street level at the rear of the building. Parking here is available only further up on S.W. Gibbs.

❦ If you're walking from the School of Nursing steps, simply cross the street to the footbridge. The long footbridge will take you to the back of the BICC Building and the beginning of the stairs will be to your right.

❦ The first set of 24 stairs takes you to the lower second story of the BICC Building. Keep following the stairs around down the outside of the building. A group of 62 stairs will take you down to a gravel path. You'll then be confronted by four hefty satellite dishes along the path. Follow the gravel path to your left and soon you'll see an older stairway on your right. These 45 stairs will take you to the back door of the Sports and Fitness Center. Continue to the left along a concrete path. There are 27 more stairs and then the remaining set of nine stairs will take you to the front of the building on S.W. Campus Drive.

Southwest Portland *OHSU*

*This is just one of the many OHSU parking structures that comes
fully equipped with stairs.*

Southwest Portland *OHSU*

BICC Building to the S.W. Campus Drive Parking Structure
Year Built: Unknown
Number of Stairs: 154
Top Locator: 3300 S.W. Sam Jackson Park Road (rear of BICC Building)
Bottom Locator: West Parking Structure on S.W. Campus Drive
Thomas Guide: 626, E-2

Directions: From Pioneer Square (S.W. Broadway and S.W. Yamhill), take
S.W. Broadway due south through downtown and past Portland State
University. As you go over I-405, S.W. 6th turns into S.W. Terwilliger. At the
second light, instead of turning left up the hill on S.W. Terwilliger Blvd.,
continue straight ahead and you'll be on S.W. Sam Jackson Park Road.
Follow the road up the hill and the BICC Building (Biomedical Information
Communications Center) will be at the crest of the hill on your left. The
stairs begin on the street level at the rear of the building. Parking here is
available only further up on S.W. Gibbs.

❦ If you're walking from the School of Nursing steps, simply cross the street
to the footbridge. The footbridge will take you to the back of the BICC
Building and the beginning of the stairs will be to your right.

❦ The first set of 24 stairs takes you to the lower second story of the BICC
Building. Keep following the stairs around down the outside of the
building. A group of 62 stairs will take you down to a gravel path. Instead of
following the gravel path to your left and down to the Sports and Fitness
Center, go to the right. You'll find a set of 56 stairs to the right that will take
you down to the mouth of the S.W. Campus Parking structure.

❦ If you want to make your way back up to the south side of the footbridge,
walk across the parking entrance and take the stairs that go up the other
side of parking structure. Go up the stairs and continue along the bark trail.
This stair adds another 54 stairs to the trip.

Southwest Portland *Terwilliger*

S.W. Terwilliger Blvd. around 1915

Southwest Portland *Terwilliger*

S.W. Terwilliger Boulevard up to S.W. Bancroft Street
Year Built: Unknown
Number of Stairs: 35
Top Locator: 348 S.W. Bancroft St.
Bottom Locator: Corner of S.W. Terwilliger Blvd. and S.W. Bancroft St.
Thomas Guide: 626, E-3

Directions: From Pioneer Square (S.W. Broadway and S.W. Yamhill), take S.W. Broadway due south out of downtown and past Portland State University. As you go over 405, S.W. 6th turns into S.W. Terwilliger. To head up the hill, get in the left-hand turn lane and make a left at the intersection of S.W. Sam Jackson Park Road and S.W. Terwilliger. The stairs are about an 1/8 of a mile past S.W. Veterans Hospital Rd.

Southwest Portland *Terwilliger*

The Nebraska Stairs

Southwest Portland *Terwilliger*

S.W. Barbur Blvd. up to S.W. Parkhill Drive
Year Built: Around 1950
Number of Stairs: 133
Top Locator: 6442 S.W. Parkhill Drive
Bottom Locator: S.W. Barbur Blvd. and S.W. Parkhill Drive
Thomas Guide: 596, E-5

Directions: From Pioneer Square (S.W. Broadway and S.W. Yamhill), take S.W. Broadway south through town. Once you pass through Portland State University, follow the signs to S.W. Barbur Blvd. You have to make a strategic jog over I-405 onto S.W. 6th Ave. Just follow the signs to S.W. Barbur Blvd. and you'll be fine. The kelly-green YMCA building and track will be on the right once you're on S.W. Barbur Blvd. Continue along S.W. Barbur, past the Capitol Hwy. turnoff. The next available turnoff to your right will be S.W. Parkhill Drive. The turnoff is about 2 1/2 miles from the YMCA building. Make a right on S.W. Parkhill Drive. This narrow street will wind up the hill and just past S.W. Nebraska St., S.W. Parkhill Drive will turn back down and you'll see the top of the stairs on your right.

❦ The neighborhood refers to this stairway as the "Nebraska Stairs." It's definitely the most expedient route to get down the hill to catch the Barbur Blvd. bus. Our Great Aunt Betty, who never learned to drive, would venture out from her Laurelhurst home to visit my Uncle's family who live just off S.W. Nebraska. She'd take the Glisan bus downtown, transfer to the S.W. Barbur bus and get off at the stop right at the base of the stairs. Even into her 60's, Aunt Betty would trot effortlessly up these stairs all the while whistling Gaudeamus Igatur.

Southwest Portland *Terwilliger*

A Spiral Sculpture

Southwest Portland *Terwilliger*

Recycled Stairs

This graceful spiral stairway (opposite page) is a special entry. It's the only private stairway in the entire book. At one time, however, these steep, potentially ankle-wrenching stairs, were very public. Anyone who had business at the Old Clock Tower at S.W. Sixth and S.W. Alder was acquainted with these stairs. When the Tower was razed in 1951, Portlanders Earl and Margaret Dubois, were bent on rescuing the stairway from ruin. At their own expense, the couple arranged to have the entire 18-foot staircase transported from downtown to their S.W. Parkhill Way home. The porch on the east side of the Dubois home was rebuilt to accommodate the three-story high corkscrew stairs where they happily remain to this day.

River Front Portland *Willamette River Bridges*

"Bridgetown, U.S.A."

Portland may be renowned for its brews and bookstores, but it's our bridges that can claim international fame. Double vertical lift bridge, double-leaf Strauss bascule, suspension and stiffened truss bridges are engineer-speak for the respective designs of the Steel Bridge, the Burnside Bridge, St. Johns Bridge and the Fremont Bridge. These and other bridges spanning the mighty Willamette represent a wondrous display of engineering ingenuity by world-renowned engineers. Golden Gate Bridge engineer Joseph Strauss designed the Burnside Bridge's massive opening mechanism. New York's commissioner of bridges, Gustav Lindenthal, drew up the plans for an upside-down version of his Queensboro Bridge in Manhattan. The result is the Ross Island bridge. Other brilliant, turn-of-the-century bridge engineers also contributed their talents. There was a collective intrigue among engineers about the variations of depth and width of the Willamette River. These variables entertained the notion of different bridge paradigms depending on the proposed location. From 1904 to 1982, a bridge has been constructed every decade. The collection of 10 bridges — 11 if you count the Railroad Bridge—represent evolving technology, making Portland truly a bridge museum. Patrons of such a museum come from all over the world to view these functional treasures. Henry Petroski, author of *Engineers of Dreams, Great Bridge Builders and the Spanning of America*, never misses a chance to stroll across the Hawthorne Bridge when he's in town. After all, it's the oldest operating vertical lift bridge in the United States.

To learn more about our bridges, pick up *The Portland Bridge Book* (Oregon Historical Society Press, ©1989) by Sharon W. Wood. She has written the consummate treatment on Portland's bridges and the drawings by Jay Dee Alley are excellent. If you want to widen your scope even further, look for Mr. Petroski's book, *Engineers of Dreams, Great Bridge Builders and the Spanning of America*. The book is packed with facts and peppered with human interest stories of bickering and general misbehaving among the country's most renowned early 20th century bridge engineers.

River Front Portland *Willamette River Bridges*

Several bridges across the Willamette are vital to non-motorists who bike, skate, walk, jog or wheel their way to and from downtown Portland. While not all bridges provide adequate accessibility, Multnomah County is currently implementing a project that includes building more stairways and ramps up to the bridges and designating more bike lanes on bridge ramps and on the bridges themselves.

Presently, the bridge stairs most frequently used are also the most abused. The litter, eau de urine and discarded syringes are sure signs of urban blight. Some stairways are appreciably better than others and they're still some of the most direct routes to get up to the bridges themselves.

Currently seven bridges provide stair access for pedestrians: (from north to south) St. Johns Bridge, Broadway Bridge, Steel Bridge, Burnside Bridge, Morrison Bridge, Hawthorne Bridge and Sellwood Bridge. In the same way that each bridge is architecturally distinct, the "stairtecture" also varies from bridge to bridge.

River Front Portland *Willamette River Bridges*

St. Johns Bridge

Saint Johns Bridge

Saint Johns Bridge is the most graceful of all the bridges that span the Willamette River. This majestic suspension bridge opened for business in 1931 and is unique among the Portland bridges for three reasons. First, St. John's Bridge is Portland's only suspension bridge; second, it's also the highest bridge suspended above the Willamette River (205 feet); and third, it boasts the longest span of any Portland bridge at 2,067 feet. The suspension cables of the St. Johns Bridge are unusual because they're actually made up of separate cables, each weighing six and a half tons. The main cable is ninety-one separate cables; that pencils out to 1,183,000 pounds. It's remarkable to think that this tonnage of suspension cables actually stretches several feet when heated by the summer sun.

When the bridge was first completed and paint color was discussed, there was talk of painting the bridge span yellow and black. Concerned with possible airplane collisions, aviation and government officials thought this paint scheme would remedy the problem. The county commissioners kindly disregarded the recommendation and announced on St. Patrick's Day that the bridge would be painted green.

Saint Johns Bridge was named for the community of St. Johns, home of the Roosevelt High School "Roughriders." The name of the community has little to do with anything saintly. St. Johns was named in honor of pioneer James Johns who came from Missouria and settled in Portland in the mid-1800's. Characterized as a recluse, Johns had many monikers, including Saint Johns. Despite his hermit ways, Johns operated a country store and went into the ferry business in 1852 with one row boat.

River Front Portland *Willamette River Bridges*

The St. Johns Bridge Stairs.

River Front Portland *Willamette River Bridges*

St. Johns Bridge Stairs
N.W. Bridge Avenue to Saint Helens Road
Year Built: Around 1930
Number of Stairs: 70
Top Locator: N.W. Bridge Ave. and N.W. Springville Rd. intersection
Bottom Locator: Saint Helens Rd.
Thomas Guide: 565, F-4

Directions: From Pioneer Square (S.W. Broadway and S.W. Morrison St.), take S.W. Morrison St. west up to S.W. 10th Ave. Turn right on S.W. 10th, then make a left onto W. Burnside St. Turn right just past S.W. 14th Ave. and get on I-405 due north. As you pass through the Pearl District and Northwest Portland, follow signs to Hwy 30. This highway is N.W. Saint Helens Rd. Take N.W. Saint Helens Rd. north past St. Johns Bridge. Follow signs for N.W. Germantown Rd. Get into the left lane and make hard left up the hill. Now you're on N.W. Bridge Ave. The stairs are on the left or east side of the road, south of N.W. Springville Road.

❦ Parking is impossible here. There's a steep little street off of N.W. Bridge Ave. called Springville Rd. where you can park. You can also take in an odd, roadside attraction — a old, dry-docked fishing boat. Once you've parked, head back down the street to N.W. Bridge Ave. and walk up towards the bridge. There's a path on the east side of the street; same side of the street as the stairway. Walk up towards the bridge and just at the beginning of the viaduct, you'll see the stairs to your left.

❦ This abandoned stairway takes you down a dirt road that winds past a lonely grey house backed up against the hill. Below the viaduct, you're confronted with towering columns of crumbling concrete above you. If, for an instant, you can possibly ignore the drone of traffic and block out any thoughts of seismic activity, you'll sense an eerie mystic quality to the setting.

River Front Portland *Willamette River Bridges*

If you can't go by train, go by the Broadway Bridge Stairs.

River Front Portland *Willamette River Bridges*

Broadway Bridge Stairs
Year Built: 1911
Number of Stairs: 82 (north side) 81 (south side)
Top Locator: Northwest side of bridge
Bottom Locator: Albers Mill on Naito Pkwy.
Thomas Guide: 596, F-4

Directions: From Pioneer Square (S.W. Broadway and S.W. Yamhill), if you're walking, head due east towards the river down to Waterfront Park. Turn north or left once you hit the promenade. You'll pass the Morrison, Burnside and Steel Bridges. Immediately upon passing under the Steel Bridge, take the Greenway Trail that runs along the river. The Broadway Bridge is straight ahead. The Greenway Trail will take you to the parking lot of Albers Mill. At this point, walk west across the parking lot to Naito Pkwy. The stairs are right across the street.

If you're driving from Pioneer Square, take S.W. Yamhill St. due east to S.W. 3rd Ave. Turn right on S.W. 3rd Ave. and then make a left onto S.W. Salmon St. Turn left on Naito Pkwy. As you pass under the Steel Bridge, Union Station will be on your left. The south set of stairs is on the west or right side of the street. The north set of stairs is just to the other side of the bridge. Parking is a challenge during the work week. There is metered parking in Old Town. China Town is also worth a shot.

❦ The color of brick red never looked better on a bridge. Built between 1911 and 1913, Broadway Bridge is a rare example of a double-leaf Rall-type bascule (French translation: seesaw). At the time of construction, Broadway Bridge was the longest double-leaf bascule drawbridge in the world. With a span length in 1736 feet, the Broadway Bridge remains the sixth longest bascule-type bridge in the states and the seventh longest in the world. The two identical stairways gracefully branch out toward the street from the bridge; one to the north, the other to the south. The pipe railings are so big and fat that you feel like a kid struggling to get an adequate grip. Great view of Union Station and the "Go By Train" sign from the bridge.

River Front Portland *Willamette River*

Broadway Bridge

River Front Portland *Willamette River Bridges*

Albers Mills by the Broadway Bridge

In 1918, at the height of anti-German sentiment in America, an unfortunate event occurred to a prosperous Portland German immigrant. J. Henry Albers was president of Albers Brothers Milling Company, a well-respected business man and an honored member of the Milwaukie, Oregon Elks Lodge. On his way back from a business trip in San Francisco, Albers whiled away the hours in the lounge car of the train. He ended up in his cups and proceeded to entertain himself by bellowing songs from his beloved Germany. Some passengers took great exception to, what they considered, obvious anti-American behavior. When Albers got off the train in Portland, he was met by the police who arrested him and threw him in jail. Albers was convicted for seditious conduct, sentenced to three years in a federal penitentiary and fined $10,000. Albers appealed his case all the way to the Supreme Court. Just prior to the hearing, the Solicitor General determined that errors had been made during the initial proceedings of the case and Albers was set free. Despite being cleared of all charges, the once vital and respected Albers was now a broken man. The final insult came when he was kicked out of the Elks Lodge. Albers had a stroke and died 10 days later.

River Front Portland ***Willamette River Bridges***

The Steel Bridge

River Front Portland *Willamette River Bridges*

Steel Bridge Stairs
Year Built: Unknown
Number of Stairs: 59 (bridge to street); 22 (connecting ramp)
Top Locator: West side of Steel Bridge
Bottom Locator: Naito Pkwy.
Thomas Guide: 596, F-5

Directions: From Pioneer Square (S.W. Broadway and S.W. Yamhill St.), if you're walking, go east towards the river down to Waterfront Park. Turn north or left once you hit the promenade. You'll pass the Morrison and Burnside Bridges. The Steel Bridge will be right in front of you. The stairs are on the south side, to the left of the spindly, shiny aluminum sculpture.

If you're driving from Pioneer Square, take S.W. Yamhill St. due east to S.W. 3rd Ave. Turn right on S.W. 3rd Ave. and then make a left onto S.W. Salmon St. Turn left on Naito Pkwy. As you pass under the Burnside Bridge, the next bridge you'll see is the Steel Bridge. Metered parking due west in Old Town or China Town is your only hope.

❦ The Steel Bridge is a double-decker vertical lift bridge, meaning the top and bottom decks lift independently of each other. Opened in 1888, the Steel Bridge remains the second oldest vertical lift bridge in North America. The span length is 1,624 feet and the bottom deck is only 26 feet above water. In 1922, the top deck opened 1,000 times a year versus about 150 times in 1996. The bottom train deck opened a whopping 20,000 times a year versus about 5,000 times today. Fewer lifts indicate that most river commerce takes place further up the river and downtown water traffic is more of a recreational nature.

❦ The Steel Bridge is grand but the stairs are a fright. The stench of urine, broken glass, etc. spell urban blight. Still, people walk the stairs every day. My advice? Hold your nose and watch your step.

River Front Portland *Willamette River Bridges*

There's always time for a bridge lift.

River Front Portland *Willamette River Bridges*

Burnside Bridge Stairs
Year Built: 1995
Number of Stairs: 30 (north side) 30 (south side)
Top Locator: West side of Burnside Bridge
Bottom Locator: S.W. First Ave. and Naito Pkwy.
Thomas Guide: F-5

Directions: From Pioneer Square (S.W. Broadway and S.W. Yamhill St.) if you're walking, go east towards the river down to Waterfront Park. Turn north or left once you hit the promenade. You'll pass the Morrison Bridge and the next bridge will be the Burnside Bridge. To get to the base of the stairs, cross Naito Pkwy. under the bridge and the stairs are on the west side of the street, straight across from the trolley stop.

If you're driving from Pioneer Square, take S.W. Yamhill St. due east to S.W. 3rd Ave. Turn right on S.W. 3rd Ave. and then make a left onto S.W. Salmon St. Turn left on Naito Pkwy. The Burnside Bridge is the second bridge to the north. Parking is nonexistent here. Your best bet is to turn left on S.W. Ankeny St. and pray for metered parking.

❦ The Burnside Bridge is a shining example of a double-leaf Strauss bascule bridge. Built between 1892 and 1894, it is the fourth oldest bridge in Portland. Some reconstruction of the bridge was performed in 1926. The span length of the Burnside Bridge is 855 feet and it sits 64 feet above water.

❦ This side of the Burnside Bridge is Saturday Market territory, so the stairs are well used on the weekend. At the top of the stairs is an aluminum banner archway — flanked by waving red flags frozen in aluminum — reads "Portland Saturday Market." Built in 1995, both the north and south stairways improve access to the open-air market, a place where you can gorge on elephant ears and find a tie-dyed tuxedo shirt.

❦ Under the east side ramp of the Burnside Bridge is a bona fide skate board park. It may look like a graffiti, fire-bombed Dresden but it's all legit.

River Front Portland *Willamette River Bridges*

The Morrison Bridge

River Front Portland *Willamette River Bridges*

Morrison Bridge Stairs
Year Built: Unknown
Number of Stairs: 23
Top Locator: West side of Morrison Bridge (eastbound on-ramp)
Bottom Locator: Naito Pkwy.
Thomas Guide: 596, F-6

Directions: From Pioneer Square (S.W. Broadway and S.W. Yamhill), if you're walking, go east towards the river down to Waterfront Park. Turn north or left once you hit the promenade. The Morrison Bridge is the first bridge to your left. To get to the base of the stairs, cross Naito Pkwy. under the bridge and you'll see the stairs on the west side of the street, straight across from the trolley stop.

If you're driving from Pioneer Square, take S.W. Yamhill St. due east to S.W. 3rd Ave. Turn right on S.W. 3rd Ave. and then make a left onto S.W. Salmon St. Turn left on Naito Pkwy. The Morrison Bridge is the first bridge ahead of you. The base of the stairs is on the west side of the street, straight across from the trolley stop. There's metered parking and some parking lots west of the bridge.

❦ Built in 1887, the Morrison Bridge is the oldest bridge in Portland. If this double-leaf Strauss bascule bridge doesn't appear to have aged in 110 years, it's because the bridge was all but replaced in 1958. Distinguishing features of the Morrison Bridge are few, save for the twin tower kiosks that look suspiciously like prison guard shacks. At night, however, the bridge is bathed in a warm glow of pink, purple and turquoise lights. Thank you Willamette Light Brigade.

❦ The stairs on this side of the river don't bring much attention to themselves but they do serve to get you up and down from the Light Rail stop. The two additional sets of stairs on the eastbound on-ramp give pedestrians a lift up to the east side of the bridge.

River Front Portland *Willamette River Bridges*

The Oregonian Printing Press Park

One street over from the S.W. 1st and S.W. Alder stairs is *The Oregonian* Printing Press Park. This tiny little park marks the exact location of the one-story wooden structure that housed *The Oregonian's* first printing press. The plaques are replicas of historic front pages of *The Oregonian*. The first plaque is a reprint of the first issue, dated December 4, 1850. That year, Portland's population was a booming 760. Each plaque recollects times of infamy or joy — the end of World War I, the assassination of Kennedy and Americans walking on the moon, to name a few.

"This park and plaques commemorate the role of The Oregonian *in the history of Portland and the Pacific Northwest."*

River Front Portland *Willamette River Bridges*

Morrison Bridge Stairs
Year Built: Around 1994
Number of Stairs: 43
Top Locator: S.E. Belmont St. off-ramp
Bottom Locator: Corner of S.E. Water Ave. and S.E. Belmont St.
Thomas Guide: 596, G-6

Directions: From Pioneer Square (S.W. Broadway and S.W. Yamhill St.) take S.W. Yamhill St. due east to S.W. 3rd Ave. Turn right on S.W. 3rd Ave. and then make a left onto S.W. Salmon St. Turn left on Naito Pkwy and follow the signs to the Morrison Bridge. There's a left-turn lane for the on-ramp to the bridge. Go over the Morrison Bridge and make sure you're in the right-hand lane so you can exit on S.E. Water Ave. There will be a stop sign at the bottom of the ramp at S.E. Water. Make a left. The stairs are on the left or west side of the street at the corner of S.E. Water and S.E. Belmont. Parking isn't a problem here.

❦ Located on the southeast side of the bridge, these concrete and aluminum stairs are steep and deliberate. If a more gradual ascent or descent is your preference, a spiral pedestrian ramp is available closer to the river. The spiral ramp was built in 1961 as part of a beautification movement and also to make pedestrian access on the eastside waterfront as viable as it is on the west side. Because the eastside waterfront has traditionally been an industrial area, establishing green spaces and a Greenway Trail-like route along the river continues to be a challenge.

❦ Similar sets of stairs can also be found at S.E. Water Ave. and S.E. Belmont St. These stairs will take you up to the westbound ramp of the Morrison Bridge. Another stairway will take you under the westbound ramp to a short path that leads to another set of 24 stairs. These stairs will take you up to the northbound ramp. Major freeway artery activity promotes much whizzing on the ramps. Should you become disoriented by exhaust fumes, the nearby Nor'wester Brew Pub is a recommended sanctuary.

Riverfront Portland *Willamette River Bridges*

The Hawthorne Bridge

Hawthorne Bridge Stairs
Year Built: Unknown
Number of Stairs: 36 stairs (north side); 37 stairs (south side)
Top Locator: West side of Hawthorne Bridge
Bottom Locator: Waterfront Park Promenade and S.W. Madison St.
Thomas Guide: 596, F-7

Directions: From Pioneer Square (S.W. Broadway and S.W. Yamhill St.), if you're walking, go east towards the river down to Waterfront Park. Turn south or right once you hit the promenade. The first bridge to the south is the Hawthorne Bridge.

If you're driving from Pioneer Square, take S.W. Yamhill St. due east to S.W. 3rd Ave. Turn right on S.W. 3rd Ave. and then make a left onto S.W. Salmon St. Turn right on Naito Pkwy. The first bridge you see is the Hawthorne Bridge. There's limited metered parking here. The south stairs up to the Hawthorne Bridge start up next to the circular, brick Police Memorial Park. The north stairs are located on the other side of the bridge.

❦ The first Hawthorne Bridge was erected in 1891 and replaced in 1910 by the bridge we see today. This bridge is the oldest, serviceable, vertical lift highway truss bridge in the nation. Sitting only 53 feet above water, the Hawthorne Bridge is also the most frequently opened bridge in Portland, averaging 200 lifts per month. The center section of the bridge lifts with the help of two 500,000-pound reinforced concrete counterweights. The next time you find yourself sitting on the bridge during a lift — and you will — walk up as close as you can to the 165-foot steel-frame towers. This is the best vantage point to watch these massive counterweights in action.

❦ The Hawthorne Bridge also sports a number of stairways to provide access for any number of the 1,000 pedestrians crossing the bridge daily. On the west side, there are five stairways and three on the east side. Take your pick.

River Front Portland *Willamette River Bridges*

The Sellwood Bridge is not only too narrow but it's tilting.

Sellwood Bridge Stairs
Year Built: Unknown
Number of Stairs: 44 stairs
Top Locator: East side of Sellwood Bridge
Bottom Locator: 380 S.E. Spokane St.
Thomas Guide: 626, G-6

Directions: From Pioneer Square (S.W. Broadway and S.W. Yamhill St.), take S.W. Yamhill St. due east to S.W. 3rd Ave. Turn right on S.W. 3rd Ave. and then make a left onto S.W. Salmon St. At Naito Pkwy. turn right. Continue along Naito Pkwy. and follow signs to Ross Island Bridge and Lake Oswego. Get in the right lane and continue following the signs to Lake Oswego. Make a left on S.W. Curry St. and continue to your right down the hill. Once you pass under I-5, you'll be on S.W. Macadam Ave. Take S.W. Macadam Ave. for about three miles until you see signs for the Sellwood Bridge. Stay in the left lane and cross over the bridge. Once you've cross the Willamette River, take the first left, S.E. 6th Ave. You'll then make a quick left onto S.E. Spokane St. Go down the street until you see the Samtrak Station. Turn left into the parking lot and you'll see the stairs next to the Sellwood Bridge and the railroad tracks.

❦ The Sellwood Bridge opened for business in 1925 under heavy criticism that it was too narrow. It was. Portland's first fixed-span bridge was built on the heels of a juicy scandal of connivance and collusion. The incident involved three Portland county commissioners and a cabal of companies who suspiciously won the building contract for the Burnside, Ross Island and Sellwood Bridges. The scandal made daily headlines in all the papers. *The News* printed a front-page editorial on April 10, 1924 that read, "Cure that's needed for Bridge Eczema and Insurance Pimples." The offending officials were acquitted but then lost their jobs in a recall election. In the afterglow of the scandal, the new breed of county commissioners was far more concerned about saving money than listening to sound engineering advice, hence the tiny, two-lane bridge.

Southwest Portland *Downtown*

It's a quick jaunt down to the river with these stairs.

Southwest Portland *Downtown*

S.W. Harbor Way up to Naito Parkway
Year Built: 1994
Number of Stairs: 56 stairs
Top Locator: Corner S.W. Harrison and Naito Pkwy.
Bottom Locator: S.W. Harbor Wy.
Thomas Guide: 596, F-7

Directions: From Pioneer Square (S.W. Broadway and S.W. Yamhill St.), take S.W. Broadway south to S.W. Market. Turn left onto S.W. Market and go east toward the river. Once you cross Naito Pkwy., the street turns into S.W. Harbor Wy. You'll see the stairs on the right or west side of the street at the corner of S.W. Harbor Way and S.W. Montgomery. Limited parking is available on S.W. Montgomery. There's also a parking structure at the end of the street.

❦ Flanked by classic street lamps, this stairway is separated into two flights by a brick path. At the top of the stairs, there's a sign post, notifying all that the stairway is part of the Greenway Trail that runs along the downtown river front. Towards the river, you'll find the popular Esplanade lined with book stores, kite stores, coffee bars, restaurants, etc.

Southwest Portland *Downtown*

Pioneer Courthouse Square

Pioneer Courthouse Square up to S.W. Yamhill Street
Year Built: 1984
Number of Stairs: 22
Top Locator: S.W. Broadway and S.W. Yamhill St.
Bottom Locator: S.W. 6th Ave. and S.W. Yamhill St.
Thomas Guide: 596, F-7

Directions: You're there.

❦ Pioneer Courthouse Square features both brick stairs and big blue and purple tile stair ledges. The design of the stairs on the southwest side of the square, cleverly incorporates a curving ramp into the steps themselves. The stairs are meant for climbing, sitting or lounging. In fact, the stairs are like the square itself; they assume the role that they're given. So whether it's a heated political rally or the lighting of the Christmas tree, Pioneer Courthouse Square is for everyone.

❦ The site of Pioneer Courthouse Square was actually the footprint of the famed Portland Hotel. This city landmark was host to 11 presidents during more than 60 years. In 1951, sky-rocketing renovation costs prompted the unfortunate decision to raze the building. The once elegant address in the heart of Portland became home to a parking lot for 30 years. In the 70's, civic leaders began contemplating the vitality of downtown and the idea of a central gathering place was discussed. Creating an open square in the original spot of the Portland Hotel (This is also the same location of the first Portland schoolhouse — built in 1856.) was proposed, acted upon and Pioneer Courthouse Square opened in 1984. Over the years, the Square has served the City well and continues to operate as Portland's "living room."

Southwest Portland *Downtown*

The Performing Arts Center Stairs

Southwest Portland *Downtown*

S.W. Main Street up to S.W. Park Avenue
Year Built: 1987
Number of Stairs: 21 stairs
Top Locator: Corner of S.W. Park Ave. and S.W. Main St.
Bottom Locator: Corner of S.W. Broadway and S.W. Main St.
Thomas Guide: 596, F-7

Directions: From Pioneer Square (S.W. Broadway and S.W. Yamhill), take S.W. Broadway south four blocks to S.W. Main St. The stairs are on the south side of the street.

The brick stairs are an interesting contrast to the diamond-patterned walkway. The Performing Arts Center is another reason why Portland's downtown is thriving. Built in 1987, the Performing Arts Center houses four separate theatres. The glass shards hanging from the dome ceiling in the lobby reflect a colorful light and cleverly obscure the office windows above.

More Stairs For Your Climbing Enjoyment...

S.W. Barbur Blvd. up to S.W. Woods	Number of Stairs: 36
S.W. Barbur Blvd. up to S.W. Lowell	Number of stairs: 28
S.W. Barbur Blvd. up to S.W. Whitaker	Number of Stairs: 79
Naito Parkway up to S.W. Whitaker	Number of Stairs: 28
S.W. Barbur Blvd. up to S.W. Viewpoint Ter.	Number of Stairs: 30
S.W. Gibbs up to S.W. Terwilliger	Number of Stairs: 123
S.W. Custer down to S.W. Taylors Ferry Rd.	Number of Stairs: 88
S.W. Barbur Blvd. up to S.W. 5th Ave.	Number of Stairs: 36
S.W. Burlingame up to S.W. 8th Ave.	Number of Stairs: 32
S.W. Water Ave. down to S.W. Kelly Ave.	Number of Stairs: 20
S.W. Grant Ave. up to Harbor Way	Number of Stairs: 28

ABOUT THE AUTHOR...

Stefana Young has had a thing for Portland stairs ever since she was five. That's when she took her first step up the "Elevator Stairs" in the Southwest Hills. Since that time Stefana has climbed countless sets of stairs all over the country and in many parts of the world. And while great stair adventures are still keenly remembered, there is nothing quite like the familiarity of a stairway from childhood. Even after conducting two years of research on virtually every single public stair in Portland, Stefana feels the same way about the "Elevator Stairs." In fact, she has yet to tire of any of the stairs in Portland.

When Stefana isn't indulging in her stair whimsy, she dreams up schemes that will make a millions of dollars so she won't have to write any more news releases about computer widgets.

The author finds there's more than one way to skin a stair.

Notes